The Mom's Guide to a Nourishing Garden

Jen Haugen, RDN, LD

Down to Earth Dietitian

The Mom's Guide to a Nourishing Garden

ISBN: 978-0-9974490-0-6

First Printing – Trade Paperback
Published in the United States of America

To order a copy of this book, please visit:

Down to Earth Dietitian
www.jenhaugen.com

DEDICATION

To my children:

Before you were born, I dreamt of you.
When you were born, I loved you so.
As you grow, I cherish the moments we have together.
There's nothing else I would rather be.
I'm honored to be your mother.

To my husband:

You have made all my dreams come true.

ACKNOWLEDGMENTS

This book began as a whisper in my soul from the Creator of the first garden.

I want to express my overflowing gratitude to my husband who continues to believe in whatever crazy ideas I may come up with, who celebrates my accomplishments, and really has helped all of my dreams come true.

My children are my muse, inspiring me to greater things each and every day. I can only pray that following my own path will somehow inspire them to be who they are meant to be as well. Gardening with them is something I cherish every time we put our hands in the soil together.

Thank you to my parents and grandparents for spending time with me in the garden as a young girl and teaching me what it means to grow good food. You grew more than food during those years; you grew a girl whose soul was nourished by the soil.

So many of my registered dietitian colleagues have supported me throughout this process. To my aunt, Peggy Saxton, the day I spent with you so long ago changed my life's direction. Chere Bork, my coach and friend, you have allowed me to find the life I was meant to live, and I will be forever grateful. Julie Beyer, writing coach extraordinaire, thank you for the hours spent editing my book, sharing uplifting words of wisdom, and helping me see how important this work really is.

Stephanie Hofhenke, my designer, also deserves a shout out. She designed my cover and was a major help in bringing this book to life.

Finally, to all those who continue to inspire me, you know who you are.

Jen Haugen, RDN, LD
Down to Earth Dietitian

CONTENTS

CHAPTER 1

THE POWER OF A MOM

I love my mother as the trees love water and sunshine.
She helps me grow, prosper, and reach great heights.
~Terri Guillemets

When I was growing up, my mom had me fill out a scrapbook page at the end of every school year that detailed all my favorites—favorite teachers, favorite friends, favorite subjects, and favorite foods. I opened the spiral bound book, *School House Memories*, in May and recorded my thoughts, inserted my report cards, and scribbled an answer to the question, "What do you want to be when you grow up?" I never gave it too much thought until in my thirties when I started re-reading these journal entries. While the book is now tattered and barely opens without losing another page from the binding, it's filled with memories of a life that barely seems real now. Yet, through my childish scribbles, I noticed a pattern. Every year when I was asked the question about the future "me" and what I wanted to be, I wrote the same answer.

Oh, I could have chosen anything because I loved math, I loved reading, I loved writing on the typewriter, and making lists. But it all boiled down to one thing, and each year it was the same dream. What was it?

I wanted to be a mother. That's it. Just a mom. Not a doctor or an architect or a lawyer. No. My lofty dreams were to become a mother.

Of course, moms aren't "just moms." As a working mother, I've fought the "not enough" syndrome for years. I thought I needed to do more, make a difference, and be more. And I'm not talking about doing more for the people I live with, my family. No, somehow, that got derailed into being more and doing more for *other* people, and I took it to the extreme. I volunteered for committees that took me to meetings once a week. I said *"yes"* to every opportunity that came my way despite knowing it would take me away from my family. I gave up my Saturday mornings so I could help other people's kids learn how to eat better. I was overwhelmed and so was my precious family.

Although I was living a life I had essentially dreamed of, I was not being intentional about my choices to be my best as a mother. I was working a lot of evening hours as a registered dietitian at a supermarket, teaching classes to kids about cooking and gardening. It was rewarding watching boys and girls actually enjoy a bite of spinach or kale that had been used in a recipe that they had assembled. Later, when their parents picked them up, the kids couldn't wait to share a bite with mom or dad.

While I loved seeing the smiling faces of the kids who were so proud of their creations and the parents who thanked me for helping their children learn more about nutrition and being healthy, I couldn't help feeling a twinge of guilt, and that guilt followed me home. More than anything, I wanted to teach my *own* kids about cooking and gardening, but I was too tired. Mentally drained and energy deprived, I couldn't muster up any more creativity for my family.

Then one day, in one moment, I realized something. God opened my eyes to what I couldn't see in all of that busy-ness and it changed everything. There I was, a registered dietitian, and I was teaching other people's kids about food and nutrition. But who was teaching my kids? Sadly, I understood that it wasn't me, and I knew in that moment that I needed to reestablish my priorities. Needless to say, it was a turning point. There were a lot of tears.

If my guilt wasn't enough of a change-maker, I also began recalling the stories of customers I had helped in the supermarket aisles. As I walked with them on a healthy food tour, I asked about their eating habits, favorite foods, and recipes so I could help them on their journey to better health. Their responses always started with, "My mom always made <recipe>, and I still do today." Or, "My mom always bought this brand of <product>, and I still do today." Whether they had been children ten years or 50 years prior to my question, I received the same answer. Moms influence their children's food choices.

It didn't matter if those choices were for comfort, nostalgia, or just simply the notion that people learn what they live, I began to understood something big.

We tend to buy the same brands and prepare the same recipes that our mothers did.

I saw this reflected in my own life. I am the product of a working mother. I buy a certain brand of spaghetti sauce because my mom bought that brand. I buy a certain brand of cereal and still enjoy it because I grew up eating that cereal most winter mornings before school. We do what our moms did because that is what we know. But, I am here to tell you, whether you like how you were raised or not, we can all become more intentional about what we teach our children.

The lightbulb was blinking and I began to realize that moms have a lot of power. I realized that *I had a lot of power*—in my own house that is. What I was doing today with my children *did* matter. If I could only take the time, refocus my energy back to my own kids, use my creativity to garden with them, and channel my talents into cooking with my family, I could make a difference. *And that difference could live long into the future, influencing generations and creating healthy memories and habits along the way.*

We as moms hold the key to health in our family and research agrees. The Project EAT study from the

University of Minnesota noted that a mom has the biggest influence on a family's eating habits. When the mom was stressed, including working full-time hours, the number of family meals diminished, less fruits and vegetables were served, and mealtimes often consisted of fast food. There was also less dialogue between the mother and her children about developing healthy eating habits.[1]

A mother is a child's first and most influential teacher about food. (I'm not disregarding dads here who are definitely important as well!) Growing up, we watched our mothers to learn about the world, including learning how to be a mother. We learned what to eat, and we internalized the knowledge of what to feed our families in the future.

Today, our children are watching and learning from us. What do we want them to learn? Is it okay to order take-out when we don't feel like cooking despite having a pantry and freezer full of food? Is it okay to munch on high calorie, low nutrition snacks when we are feeling overwhelmed? I give these examples because I have lived them. So, rather than striving for perfection, I'm moving forward and creating a path of *intentionality* where I take time to focus on the issues that matter, like creating memories and building a healthier lifestyle that includes balance and simplicity.

Our mothers have influenced the brands we purchase, the foods we serve at mealtime, the recipes we love to make, and even our philosophy about health. It's a recipe for a legacy that started before us and will hopefully continue to live through us. What I choose to do today lives on not just with me, but with my children. I am creating a legacy as a mom, a legacy that will not only continue to influence my children, but my grandchildren, and my great-grandchildren.

As for nurturing our families by gardening? It's not a coincidence that I have a garden in my backyard. After all, my grandmothers both planted gardens in their yards, and my mother planted a garden of her own. Our mothers learned from their mother's habits, and our grandmothers learned from our great-grandmother's habits.

I believe every moment matters, and every mom matters to all those moments. Moms create moments that become lasting memories. My wish for you is that you take the time to create many mom-moments or MOMents together with your family around food.

I believe every mom can change the world and it starts right in our own homes. We are powerful, moms, pretty powerful indeed.

Moments for Mom:

List five brands of food that you purchase currently that you grew up eating:

List two ways that you are being intentional about what you are teaching your children about food:

List two ways that you think you could improve your intentionality about food:

CHAPTER 2

CONNECTING THE DOTS

Remember that children, marriages, and gardens
reflect the kind of care they receive.
~H. Jackson Brown, Jr

Remember those "connect-the-dot" puzzles you did as a child? You drew a line from dot to dot, first not knowing what the picture would become, and later, as more dots became connected, the picture became crystal clear? This puzzle played out in my life as well. Living through moments, I didn't realize they were really dots in the puzzle—the bigger picture that was my life. It wasn't until I looked back that I could see what had transpired.

My awareness of this personal "connect-the-dots" puzzle began when I started looking backward with the help of a life coach. Before you put the book down and call me crazy, I must tell you that working with a life coach was a life changing experience.

During that period of my life, I was busy beyond busy. My mind was constantly racing with new and creative ideas that I could implement at my position as a supermarket dietitian. There was no "off" switch. I was given nearly free rein over projects and freedom to do whatever I wanted to do with my time. This was a dangerous situation for a girl who wanted to make a difference by helping people—and for someone who thought she could star on the Food Network someday.

In the middle of this chaotic life, I attended the 2011 annual conference for our state's dietitians. The keynote speaker for the conference was a registered dietitian, Chere Bork, who spoke on the topic of *"Living a Value-Driven Life."* Although there were hundreds of dietitians in that large conference room, I was so drawn into her presentation that I was sure she was speaking only to me. I knew I had to find her after the seminar and share what an impact her message had on me...but when I met her, all I could do was shed tears. I was overwhelmed with the realization that the way I was living my life did not reflect my values. Chere became my life coach not long after that defining moment.

Working with a life coach is hard. It requires a lot of soul searching, and the one thing I learned from that experience was this...*to understand where you are going, you need to look backward.* So I did. And in the process I began to connect my dots...

The "Growing" Years

"Drive four miles north of Lakefield, Minnesota, turn right onto "Kilen Woods" road, and then in one mile, turn right onto the first gravel road you see. Drive up and over the hill about a half mile and on the right hand side you will see a small farm."

These are the directions I heard repeated so many times to direct visitors to our house before cell phones and GPS. Just writing those words takes me home.

Where I lived with my family was no place special, in fact it was in the middle of nowhere. While my family no longer lives there, many memories do. I grew in the soil there, nourished my roots there, and seeds were sprouting inside of me that I wouldn't be aware of for many years.

Our home was a farm on a gravel road with an old farmhouse built in the 1890's. There was a barn, a garden, and a few apple trees. An expansive lawn required three to four hours of mowing. Tractors and farm equipment filled the machine shed. Chickens lived in the chicken house, pigs in the hog barn, and a few beef cattle in the cattle yard. Flower gardens included bleeding hearts, tiger lilies, and peonies. Ferns grew on the north side of the house, and we hung our clothes on a clothesline in the backyard.

I often find myself thinking about our family garden. The garden was large by most standards, and it grew a mouthwatering variety of fruits and vegetables. Square-shaped and next to the gravel road on our farm, there were many evenings my parents, my sister, my brother, and I spent time working in the garden. It was one of my favorite activities because it was a time when the whole family was doing something together.

That family garden defined my own growing years. In every season, there was talk about the garden. Each winter, we would receive seed catalogs in the mail, and I would sit in our small living room looking at all the colorful fruits and vegetables we could grow. I made lists of what we should plant. There were cucumbers, broccoli, cauliflower, asparagus, corn, potatoes, beets, lettuce, carrots, peas, summer squash and winter squash, watermelon, cantaloupe, onions, tomatoes, peppers, and celery. As a young child, I daydreamed about how great it would be to see the snow melt and get in the garden, and while dreaming of the future harvest, I read cookbooks for fun.

In the spring when seeds were planted in the garden, deeper seeds were planted in my soul. I loved feeling the wind and warm sun on my skin. The earthy smell of the soil was refreshing as I helped plant potatoes with an old potato planter. I planted neat rows of peas by pushing the seeds of the peas down until the soil hit my knuckles. I shored up the soil around the fragile tomato plants that we had started inside the house that were now being transplanted outside into the garden.

Summer was punctuated by the harvests. The question, *"What's ready in the garden?"* was the question that dictated what was served at the next meal. This excitement over fruits and vegetables couldn't be forced; the garden allowed it to happen naturally. I would literally skip from our house to the garden across the lawn just to see if there were any fruits or vegetables to harvest. I would touch the leaves of the tomato plants or the fresh herbs growing in my little square of the garden, then bring my fingers to my nose, inhaling the smell. I planted, I weeded, I watered, I harvested. I even took the foods I grew to the county fair in the form of recipes, garden vegetable boxes, and nutrition projects.

In the fall, we put the garden to bed and preserved our food. And in the winter, we savored the flavor of the fruits and vegetables grown a few months earlier and began planning for the following year's garden. I gardened because my family did it together; it was our nightly activity after our chores were done. Our family garden was the first dot in my puzzle.

Education and Intuition

The second dot in my puzzle was my choice of career. In high school, my plan was to become an accountant; I loved the experience of making numbers balance. Or so I thought. Maybe it was the idea of achieving balance that I was drawn to. So, with some nudging from my parents, I shadowed my aunt at her job. She worked as a registered dietitian at an outpatient clinic, and I was fortunate to spend the day with her.

In those few hours, my life was changed. I listened to her counsel a patient on how to manage his diabetes through better eating habits, eating regular meals, and including fruits and vegetables at each of those meals. I heard her talk about reducing cholesterol by increasing fiber, which was naturally found in whole grains, fruits, and vegetables. And, I took note when even the youngest patient with weight issues listened intently to after-school snack ideas that were nourishing to the body. Each of these patients had something in common; they needed to make a change in what they were eating so they could regain their health. I was mesmerized by this concept.

The dots were starting to connect, and I made a life changing decision to help people live healthier lives by teaching them about food and nutrition. I was going to become a registered dietitian. (Here's the lesson, moms: expose your children to new experiences and nurture their talents and gifts. You just might help them find their passion!)

Off to college I went, studying chemistry, biology, anatomy, and physiology. I couldn't wait to take my nutrition classes so I could learn more about the interaction of nutrients on the different body systems. I began to discover why it was so important to eat the foods our bodies needed. I created recipes and attempted food experiments in my foods' lab classes. I cooked for the children's daycare that was right on campus. I loved everything about recipes—tinkering to find the right ingredients, fine-tuning the instructions, and creating a nourishing meal.

After college, I was accepted to a year-long internship at Mayo Clinic. After completing this "on the job training" and taking my board exams, I was officially a registered dietitian and could sign "RD" after my name. (Note: In 2013, the credential changed to registered dietitian nutritionist or "RDN.")

In 2001, shortly after completing my education, I began my quest to help patients live a healthier life, also at Mayo Clinic. I was ready to replicate what I had seen during my job shadowing day. From hospital room to hospital room, I worked with patients newly diagnosed with diabetes to plan meals and menus to help bring their blood sugars under control. I talked about ways to reduce sodium for patients who had undergone heart surgery. And I worked with patients who had cancer—fragile souls who wanted nothing more than to enjoy eating again. In all of these cases, as with all of the patients I saw each day, the question was the same: how could food help them achieve better health after they became ill?

Over time, an awareness of something else was developing. Many of these illnesses could be attributed to years of poor lifestyle and nutrition habits. I realized I was working on the reactive side of healthcare, and I desperately wanted to teach people what they could do *before* serious illness develops, showing them how each choice matters whether we see the outcome today or long into the future. I wanted to work on the prevention and wellness side of illness. This became another dot in the puzzle.

A Garden of Our Own

While I was working on the reactive side of healthcare, I was also planting seeds in my own garden at home. Although my husband did not experience gardening as a boy, he knew it was something I loved, so he dug a space in the yard for my own, first garden. He prepared the soil, and I planted seeds. I was excited to see if I could do this on my own! I planted tomatoes, peppers, and strawberries—all things we liked to eat—and the first season began.

Our son was born shortly after that first garden, and 21 months later, our daughter was born. We moved to make room for our growing family. I had dreamed of being a mother, and my goal was finally achieved! Even though I was occasionally uncertain of my mothering abilities, I loved this role. I couldn't wait to snuggle my kids into bed and serve them nourishing food. And I couldn't wait to garden with them.

Unfortunately, working 40 miles away meant leaving home at 6:00 a.m. and not returning until 6:00 p.m. It meant putting my kids to bed in their clothes for the following day to give them a few extra moments of sleep in the morning so they could be rested for day care. For some reason, the idea of my kids not actually sleeping in pajamas troubled me. There just wasn't enough time with my kids, especially since they were so little and their bedtimes were so early.

In those early years, I was still hungry to "do it all." Despite the fact that the only, limited time I had with my kids was on nights and weekends, I wanted to re-create some of my childhood memories by gardening as a family.

So my husband was in charge of another garden, this time raised-bed style. As soon as our kids took their first steps, I took them out to the garden. I would literally plant them into the soil, and they would feel their way around the garden, making themselves at home. These experiences formed another connection dot in my journey.

The garden grew, and so did our kids. They were excited to harvest and water the garden. They loved finding new treasures to take into the house for our meals. Some foods didn't even make it into the house! My kids would harvest and then eat snap peas and raspberries right out in the yard. When my son was able to handle a plastic knife, I had him cut up bell pepper slices with me, and I watched as he ate nearly the entire pepper himself—all because he grew it and was now cutting it up. He was experiencing this food in a whole new way.

An "A-Ha" Moment

In the summer of 2008, I was taking my 3 and 5 year old kids to swimming lessons, watching them jump in and out of the pool when something caught my eye. It was the number of kids who were heavier than what they should be. I also noticed the amount of candy being consumed at these evening lessons, right at supper time.

My dietitian brain kicked in, and I began reading articles on childhood obesity and the serious problem it was becoming. Since one of my roles as a hospital dietitian was to get people eating again because they were so sick or injured and were losing weight, I had lost touch with reality until I started to get out into my community. I didn't realize the childhood obesity problem was actually happening all around me in my own neighborhood.

I wondered about my own life experiences and whether those experiences played a role in my current eating habits. Had it made any difference? What had I gained from growing up in a garden?

- Had I gained an appreciation for fruits and vegetables and food in general because my hands were in the soil growing them?

- Did I understand as a child there was a connection between fruits and vegetables and good health?
- Did I have a good attitude about fruits and vegetables and a desire and willingness to eat them just because I grew them?

I knew without a doubt that the answer to all of those questions was a resounding, "Yes!"

But the freight train of ideas didn't stop there. The thoughts kept rolling along...

- Could my experience be translated into a garden program for kids in my community, providing an opportunity for them to learn where their food comes from and how eating fruits and vegetables can benefit their health?
- Was the answer to the community issues I was seeing found in a garden?
- Could a garden transform a child into a vegetable eater?
- Could gardening influence eating behaviors positively and for a lifetime?

God connected the dots again for me. Not by coincidence, in 2008, I applied for a new position as a supermarket dietitian where I could strive to make an impact on families before they suffered long-term lifestyle consequences. At my interview, I was asked the following question, *"What is your dream goal?"* I, of course, answered, *"To create a garden for kids in our community."*

With this new position, I had the chance to get a closer look into shopper's grocery carts and hear what they were thinking. I witnessed a shopper buying Fancy Feast® for his cat, while purchasing chips and snack cakes for himself. Then there was the day I was demonstrating "Muffin Egg Frittatas" filled with colorful peppers and onions, and I heard a mom say to her kids, "You won't like that because it has vegetables!" To combat the negativity around food, I decided to offer cooking classes for kids and begin planning for my kids' community garden.

Creativity overflowed into my cooking classes, where I covered topics like "Eat Bright," encouraging kids to eat all the colors of the rainbow and "Supermarket Smarts," where kids learned how to read labels in the grocery store and prepare healthier foods at home.

Then it came time for the garden programs, and the "Sprouts Get Out and Grow" garden was launched.

In the spring of 2011, after a year's worth of planning and community collaboration, the garden was planted. More than 150 kids, from preschool to fourth grade, attended classes that first season to get their hands in the soil, to water and weed, and to harvest and cook.

The gardening program had a simple mission statement, chosen to illustrate how simple ideas can change the course of a life. What was it? *"To plant the seeds for healthy habits that would last a lifetime."* I hoped that kids would find gardening fun, would want to do it with their families, and that they would begin to appreciate that fruits and vegetables could be tasty and flavorful to eat.

The classes included a short nutrition lesson, time spent in the garden learning about one particular plant, watering, weeding (i.e. playing "Plants and Robbers!"), and finally harvesting fresh produce that was assembled into a recipe the kids created themselves. We made things like "Chard Quesadillas" and "Fruity Chardy Salad." We cooked up

"Cauliflower Mac and Cheese" and made "MyPlate Pizza" filled with vegetables.

At the end of the season, we hosted a cooking competition we called "Cropped!"—a garden version of the popular show Chopped™—featuring the produce grown in the garden. Kids were paired with actual chefs to create MyPlate meals that included cancer-fighting ingredients. Judging took place and winners were declared. Of course, anyone who was a part of this garden was a winner!

I was starting to see that this community garden for kids was really working. One mom emailed me and said her daughter had come home very excited about Swiss chard. She was shocked! She heard from her daughter that she had eaten it in a quesadilla and then tried it in a fruit and chard salad. Her daughter loved it so much she wanted her mom to buy some Swiss chard. Not only was this mom blown away by the fact her daughter was asking for vegetables, she was also stunned that she was asking for Swiss chard—a green leafy vegetable that most kids shy away from and, quite frankly, the mom had never purchased! She wondered if this had actually happened that day in class, and I confirmed her daughter's story. I later heard that because of her daughter's request, the mom Googled Swiss chard, purchased it, and allowed her daughter to share the recipes with the rest of the family. What a fantastic learning experience not only for the daughter, but everyone!

Another example of the garden's influence took place at the end of the garden's first season. A news reporter came to find out if kids were really benefitting from this garden project. He interviewed several students who were eager to share with him everything they had learned. As he was finishing his footage, he wanted to be sure to showcase all of the vegetables growing in the garden.

But there was one problem. The reporter couldn't find the carrots. He came to me and asked where they were. I pointed. He went over. He came back. He still couldn't find them. I laughed at first, but then stopped as I realized this one situation validated all of the reasons and hours of labor that went into this garden. I had educated a community of kids who not only knew that carrots were good for them, *but they knew that carrots grew underground.*

As the popularity of this program grew, I taught others how to start gardens for kids at Hy-Vee supermarkets in the eight states of the Midwestern region. I wrote a garden manual, created lesson plans, and I mentored other dietitians via webinars. The program was an overwhelming success, and it continues today in more than 100 locations within the Hy-Vee company.

Yet, during the time I was developing the garden program, teaching hundreds of classes to kids in our community, and receiving national attention with numerous published stories, I kept feeling that it wasn't enough. There was something else tugging at my heart—my own children.

I was teaching other people's kids how to cook and garden more than I was teaching my own. Not because I didn't want to, but because I didn't have the time or energy to, or so I thought.

From Dots to a TED Talk

About the same time I had my epiphany and began working with Chere, I received a call to speak at a brand new conference in our community—an independently organized TED event. TED is an event featuring speakers who want to share ideas that can help make a difference in the world. Agreeing to this presentation was the beginning of my mission to refocus my energies and talents on being a mom to the two kids I have. My TED Talk idea? *"How Moms Can Change the World."*

I have always had this drive to change the world as a registered dietitian. I knew I wanted to do something big. I wanted to make a difference, to be remembered, and to leave a legacy. But in preparing for this TED talk, I realized I could also change the world by focusing on the world right in my own home and my own backyard. I could change the course of history if I could only spend time gardening and cooking with my own kids because then they would do it with their kids, passing on a legacy that will hopefully last generations. Doing this one simple thing could make all the difference in the world. *I had to tell myself over and over that it was enough to be a mom who teaches her kids how to grow a garden. It was enough to be a mom who cooks for her family. It was enough to be a mom and wife who cares about the health of her family and wants to create valuable memories.*

Even though it was an extremely tough decision, I left HyVee after six years to regain balance within my family. I can say with 100% confidence, that it was the best decision for me at the time. Instead of being everything to everyone, I was finally able to focus on who I needed to be to the people who mattered to me the most.

I took my own advice and got back to gardening with my family because I knew the memories made in the soil would sprout into something much more over time. I needed to believe that the memories I had from childhood would bloom into something I could share with my own family, creating a legacy I could leave for them—a legacy of simplicity, balance, fun, health, and satisfying contentment.

As moms, we can change the world we live in by starting with the simple idea of gardening with our kids as a family. We can create an intentional time where we work together in the garden, bond over broccoli, connect over carrots, and sow memories into the soil of our souls.

Changing the world as a mom means changing our mindset, realizing that what we have is enough, and understanding that small, simple memories can make the biggest differences in our family life.

Imagine your kids running out of the car as soon as it's parked to go and check the garden. Imagine your kids harvesting peas, shelling them, and eating them before they even make it into the house. Imagine a life of soul-satisfying growth happening all around you. That's what a garden can do. It can allow you to become a more intentional mother, a mother that lives her values, and a mother that wants to leave a legacy her kids will always want to remember.

Mom, you CAN change the world!

Moments for Mom:

What dots in your past can you connect to where you are today?

What's your food history? Did you garden growing up? Did you cook growing up? What are your favorite memories around food from your childhood?

What is the legacy you want to leave your children? What do you want to be remembered for?

CHAPTER 3

CREATING THE RECIPE TO A NOURISHING LIFE

*It is the sweet, simple things of life
which are the real ones after all.* ~Laura Ingalls Wilder

I can vividly remember being seven years old and pulling open the squeaky kitchen drawer to look for the recipe to "Grandma's Chocolate Chip Cookies" in the well-loved pages of our church cookbook. Just as that young girl yearned for that one perfectly sweet recipe, later in life I began to search for the perfect recipe I could use to create a more nourishing life.

You see, ever since I realized that I was not living the life I intended when I wrote down my dreams in that scrapbook so long ago, I decided I needed a new recipe which included nurturing my family, creating a sense of balance in every day, living out my purpose, and focusing on health and spirituality. It was a recipe I desperately needed.

As I was looking for something to define the life I craved, I needed to sketch out my values and priorities. I was looking for connection and direction. I didn't want perfection. I wanted time to connect with my family. I wanted to be their teacher and create memories with them. I knew I wanted more time and less hurry. I wanted to make more intentional choices and to stop sacrificing myself and my family to meet someone else's schedule and expectations based on *their* values and priorities.

There are times when our lives feel dull and depleted and there are times when our lives are vibrant with abundance. Where do you stand right now? Are you living a life of feeling depleted or are you living a life of abundance? Once again, a garden can show us the way, illustrating what it looks like to live a life feeling depleted, with nothing more to give, or demonstrating to us what it looks like to have enough and live a fulfilled life of abundance.

A Tale of Two Gardens

One year we planted three rows of sweet corn in our freshly tilled garden. The soil was black and looked rich with nutrients. The seeds began to germinate and grow just like any other seeds in our garden that year. But there was something a bit off balance that season. The taller the stalks grew, the more yellow the leaves became. The plants were experiencing signs of stress. They were lacking something.

Despite this stress, ears of corn started to develop once the stalk was tall enough, but when we harvested those ears, they were only half-full with corn kernels, and many of the ears were deformed. The corn stalks tried to produce the kernels they were genetically capable of, but without the right nutrients and nourishment, they just couldn't. Although the garden appeared well nourished at the beginning of the season, it didn't take long for it to show what truly wasn't in the soil. Spent and depleted, this soil hadn't received what it should have, and it didn't have anything more to give.

Contrast that to the year we grew cherry tomatoes. These weren't just any cherry tomatoes, they were the variety "Sweet 100." You can guess what the 100 might mean. The area where we grew these tomatoes was a former site of a rabbit cage, and the soil was fertile and rich with nutrients. These plants produced almost effortlessly to the point of overabundance because they were in well-cared for soil. With adequate water and sunlight, the soil allowed the tomato plants to thrive, and we shared gallon size buckets of tomatoes with our neighbors. We began to recognize the power of nourishing the garden, ensuring that the right nutrients were in abundance for the seeds to sprout and produce the fruits and vegetables we loved to eat.

Do you feel more like the yellowing corn stalk with half-full ears of corn trying to produce what you can but because you are stressed you aren't able to live well? Or are you growing something well and in abundance, like the cherry tomatoes? Are you depleted and spent with nothing more to give, or are you overflowing with creativity and gratitude? Do you feel well-nourished and well-cared for, or do you feel like you are spending the last of what you have on others without any reserves for yourself?

For me, this recipe ebbs and flows. At times I feel like I am living in abundance and filled with gratitude. Then there are times where I'm living stressed and overwhelmed. But the one thing I've discovered is what's good for the garden, is also good for us. There's an essential garden ingredient that is life-giving and has to be added frequently. That same ingredient can be applied to our lives as well.

That ingredient is *compost*. We add compost to gardens to supply crucial nutrients that all plants need, while adding organic matter, loosening the soil, and making the soil easier to handle. When compost is added to a garden, plants will be stronger and able to withstand the stresses of the growing season because soil with added compost has the ability to hold water better for the plants to draw from during dry spells. Compost also improves the structure of the soil while supporting millions of living organisms beneath the ground. I love that compost also helps reduce harmful weeds and pathogens, allowing the garden to thrive, and it offers a buffer to chemical imbalances in the soil, helping the plants flourish.

Could adding the right ingredients create a recipe for a more nourishing life? Is there a compost recipe that we can use to help us create a more intentional life—a life that perhaps got away from us and we are trying to reclaim?

I would like to share a recipe for compost that we all can use to enrich the soil of our lives. This recipe is simple, yet it does require a bit of work. If we want to thrive and grow and help our families flourish, then we must apply this recipe for compost to our lives. Without it, life will get swept away so quickly, we will wonder what happened.

Compost: A Recipe for Life

Here is what I've discovered the recipe to be. Just for fun, and hopefully to help you remember, I will use the letters in the word "compost" to guide you, so you can create a personalized recipe for a more nourishing life. Those words are:

C – Create intention

O – Observe life

M – Make margins

P – Prune and weed

O – On purpose living

S – Surround yourself with "compost people"

T – Take the "Ten Year Soul Test"

Create intention. You want to create an intentional life, not be constrained by a tightly compacted schedule. That means creating a life that's connected to those people who matter to you the most. To do this, you must list who those people are, answering the question, *"Who do I want to have a relationship with the most?"* To become more intentional, you must be deliberate with your choices and deliberate with your schedule. By being strategic with your choices, you will begin to live the life *you* were meant to live, not the life others want you to live. Practice saying *"yes"* to those things that matter to you most and saying *"no"* to the things that really don't reflect your values or nurture you and your family. If you aren't sure at first, remember, it's okay to pause and respond later.

Observe life. Take time to observe life to find joy and contentment, fostering an appreciation for everything you have been given. Slow down and savor the moments. Wake up with an attitude of gratitude each day and dread will naturally be minimized. Record your gratefulness daily in some way—in your calendar, in a journal, or on a white board. Gratitude builds patience, joy, and contentment.

Make margins. Making a margin is about creating a buffer and establishing white space. It gives you permission to take time for yourself. If the words in this book were spread all the way to the binding, or they were written right off the page, the book would be nearly impossible to read. White space around the words brings things into balance.

Where is the white space in your life? Is it in your morning routine? Is it in the evening when the kids have gone to bed? Or maybe it's in the bathroom because you can lock the door. Wherever it is, it doesn't matter. It's more important just to have the space to do nothing and just "be." If your family schedule keeps you running off the page, so to speak, it will be hard to live with intention. Establishing a buffer will help you create a more nourishing life.

Prune and weed. After you have set your intentions, or decided what you really want for your life, and then you have observed joy and gratitude and defined a margin for yourself, the next step is to prune and weed.

Pruning and weeding a garden creates new growth, and it can do the same for your life. When you prune, it may feel as if you are cutting away something important, and you may wonder what the final outcome will be. Yet, through pruning, the growth becomes more vigorous and the plant is able to sustain itself better and thrive.

What does pruning and weeding your life look like? It looks like saying the word "no" when you really want to say "yes." It looks like cutting out the things you may have been involved with for too long. It looks like trimming back your commitments so you can have more time with your family. It might also mean removing the weeds from your life, those things that you know aren't good for you, but you keep doing anyway. Removing those weeds can restore joy and energy to your life so you can nurture yourself and your family.

On purpose living. Hopefully by now, you have decided that you want to create a life of living on purpose—living your life to match your values. My values are health, family, spirituality, purpose or meaning, and balance. Once I discovered these values, it was much easier to know which activities fit and which ones were cluttering my personal recipe for a nourishing life. I shifted and pruned until the life I was living matched those values. Although it may be hard at times, the rewards are great. When your actions begin to complement your values, your life becomes more balanced, fruitful, and feels peaceful.

Surround yourself with "compost people."
Adding compost to the garden enriches what is
already in the soil. Adding compost to your life
includes paying attention to the people you surround
yourself with. Good "compost people" are supportive,
they listen, and they are interested in your life.
Compost people are enthusiastic and grateful. They
are people who aren't afraid to be who they really are.

When you surround yourself with people who you
aspire to be like, people who share your values, you
become more like them. On the flip side, when you
spend time with people who are negative, who make
poor choices, or who are afraid to make decisions out
of fear, you may find yourself thinking more
negatively and becoming more fearful. I believe the
people we surround ourselves with are the people we
become. Choose your compost people carefully.

Take the "Ten Year Soul Test." While healthy
gardens benefit from "soil tests" to assess the health of
the earth, you can also do a "soul test," or assessment,
to make sure the right ingredients are in your soul to
create the legacy you want to leave. To do this, list out
what you want for yourself in ten years. Using as
much description as possible, visualize where you

want to be, who you want to be with, and what you want your life to look and feel like. Then measure your life where you are right now against the ten year visualization you have created. Are you headed where you want to grow? If not, this is your chance to reset the direction of your legacy.

The last few years of my life have been about finding my way back to the garden and the simple idea of adding compost. This compost recipe has become my recipe for creating a more nourishing life. It's helped me find the balance I need, and it's helped me feel nourished. It's helped me create the life I've always wanted instead of living by someone else's expectations. It's helped me become more of the mom I've always wanted to be.

Gardening has helped me create this recipe. It's helped me create balance and simplicity, and it now includes the things I craved most when my life was spinning out of control. It's helped me appreciate the value of slowing down and savoring the small moments, and it has given me time to treasure the extraordinary moments in ordinary days. Take some time to think about the compost recipe in your life. It's an essential ingredient in a more nourishing life.

Create Your Recipe to a Nourishing Life:

Adding compost to your life is essential. Describe the life's vision you intend to create:

How do you observe your life each day? What brings you the most joy?

Where are the margins in your life? What space in your schedule allows for time for yourself and time as a family?

What are your top five values? To figure these out, use the resource in the Appendix.

What parts of your life do you need to prune so more important things can thrive?

Who are your "compost" people—those who help you grow?

Take a few minutes to think about the "Ten Year Soul Test." How can you align your life with those goals?

CHAPTER 4

GARDENING:
AN INGREDIENT IN THE RECIPE

The glory of gardening: hands in the dirt, head in the sun, heart with nature. To nurture a garden is to feed not just the body, but the soul. ~Alfred Austin

Gardens not only nourish us with food, but they also nourish our souls. We may be planting broccoli seedlings, but we are also planting memories. We may have harvested carrots, yet, we have also harvested connection. We may have watered the tomatoes, but we have also watered and cared for each other. And while we may have weeded the strawberry patch, we've also helped one another weed out what doesn't belong in our lives. Gardens are deeply nourishing.

My mother gardens because it brings her life back into focus and connects her to the earth. Gardening is therapy for her soul. When I asked her why it was so important for her to include her kids in the garden, she shared with me, *"Gardening as a family becomes a place where no one is an expert. Instead, everyone teaches each other, enjoys each other, and works side by side together. Gardening is not only a place to grow vegetables, but it's also a place to grow closer as a family."*

Gardening isn't just about growing vegetables. It's about growing closer together as a family. The vegetables grown become meals around the table. Gardening is an activity where family members can do the same work or activity together, creating and caring for something bigger than themselves. Gardening is truly a gift we can give our families.

From Mom's Intuition to Research

In a study published in the *Journal of Community Health*, researchers followed 42 families who were learning about organic gardening while working in community gardens. The researchers found that not only were families experiencing the health benefits of gardening, which included eating more vegetables, but the families also felt more unified, more bonded, and more connected, all because of gardening.[1] The researchers concluded that time spent working together in the garden boosted family unity.

Recently, my family experienced a week where there was an activity every night, and things couldn't have felt more chaotic. Sleep schedules, communication, and family meals were disrupted. I couldn't help but wonder that if this were our normal weekly schedule, what would start to fail? We've all seen the realities of keeping a schedule that is too crowded. Family relationships become strained. School work is compromised because there is never enough time to complete homework. Health may fail over the long term because poor nutrition becomes routine.

There is nothing I want more for my kids than for them to be healthy. When they are healthy, they can do the things they love to do. I don't want them hindered by poor food choices. I want them to know that every choice they make can impact their health and happiness. Does that mean there aren't treats in our house? Certainly not. My kids enjoy cookies, ice cream, and chips just like other kids do. But I also realize, while it is easy to coast along each day without a second thought about how good it feels to feel good, that can be lost in an instant with a diagnosis or illness that that suddenly changes everything.

We know the positive power of frequent family meals where everyone sits around the same table, eats the same food, and enjoys each other, and I believe there is also power in family gardening.

Gardening is nutritious. Gardens give us foods that are filled with nutrients. Gardens even promote better fruit and vegetable eating habits. After all, something may get plucked from the ground and go directly into the mouth as a snack, and the time invested in the garden working with the fruits and vegetables often transforms into more nutrients on the plate. Then, without a doubt, gardening is active. Did you know that the physical exercise of weeding a garden can burn 200 to 400 calories per hour?

I love what parents shared during my time as a garden class teacher. While I worked with hundreds of children, watching their eating habits change and grow through gardening, their parents noticed changes too. When I asked those parents what they noticed about their kids and their eating habits after the classes, they shared the following:

- 52% of parents noted positive changes in attitudes about fruits and vegetables
- 61% of parents noticed increased excitement about creating a recipe together at home
- 48% of parents served more fruits and vegetables to their families
- 44% of parents cooked more frequently with their kids, and
- 33% of parents decided to plant a garden with their family.

While this was just a survey of parents with kids involved in my program, it actually reflected the research being done on a national level where kids of all ages were involved in garden programs. Research published in the *Journal of the Academy of Nutrition and Dietetics* showed that when kids were involved in gardening programs:

- 98% of those children enjoyed tasting new fruits and vegetables

- 96% of those children enjoyed working in the gardens, and
- 91% of those children actually enjoyed learning about fruits and vegetables through gardening.

In addition, when parents were asked whether having their kids involved in gardening helped the health of the family, 95% of parents answered with a resounding *"yes!"*[2] Who can argue with numbers like that? We hear stories about kids who refuse to try fruits and vegetables, yet in the majority of cases, kids who work in a garden are willing to take risks and try something new, especially when they have watched it grow and develop. Family gardening is a proven, non-threatening activity to boost your child's nutrition.

Planting the Seeds for a Healthier Life

"I know how to prevent cancer, Mom! Plant a garden and eat the rainbow!" I heard this from a mom whose daughter attended my gardening classes. How amazing is it that a young girl comprehended that nourishing her body meant to plant a garden and eat all colors of fruits and vegetables! What if all kids understood this? Maybe, it doesn't have to be so hard to get them to eat those vegetables!

What seeds can you plant in your garden to nourish your family to a healthier life? Research suggests that many chronic diseases, like diabetes, heart disease, and cancer, are related to a state of chronic inflammation. Chronic inflammation is like chronic stress on our body systems due to poor nutrition and lifestyle choices. Over time, these systems become damaged due to the stress. But the good news is that fruits and vegetables play an important role in preventing that inflammation. In an upcoming chapter, I have noted which fruits and vegetables contribute most to anti-inflammation.

Seeds for a healthy heart also include keeping blood pressure in a healthy range. Foods rich in potassium and magnesium help do this and these minerals are found in many foods we can grow in the garden. Great sources of potassium and magnesium include fruits and vegetables like tomatoes, citrus, broccoli, sweet potatoes, greens, and more.

There are also seeds we can plant for cancer prevention. Numerous studies point to a link between eating fruits and vegetables and protection against cancer. But here's where it gets a bit fuzzy. Other studies have *not* consistently shown that a diet rich in fruits and vegetables act to prevent cancer. How do we interpret this? A likely explanation is that some types of fruits and vegetables *may* protect against *certain* types of cancers. According to a report published by the World Cancer Research Fund and the American Institute for Cancer Research, the most beneficial vegetables are dark leafy greens, cruciferous vegetables (like broccoli, cabbage, cauliflower), along with garlic and onions.[3]

There are also seeds we can plant for healthy digestion. Our digestive tracts are lined with beneficial bacteria and our immunity depends on those bacteria. Our digestive tracts also need to be continually cleaned. Consider what would happen if you never swept under your cabinets where all the crumbs are. Eventually you would find giant dust bunnies under there. Keeping our guts healthy by eating fruits and vegetables not only boosts our immunity, but also reduces problems like constipation and long term issues like diverticulosis.

Finally, there are seeds we can plant for our souls and wellness—seeds of rest and recharging, of quiet and calm as well as seeds of understanding ourselves and where we belong. Gardens can provide a natural way to destress and improve mood. There is nothing like intense weeding or hoeing to help release frustrations and negative thoughts! There's definitely healing power in a garden.

Modern Day Victory Gardens

I want to give you one final thought in this chapter. As part of the war effort in the 1940s, the government rationed foods like sugar, butter, milk, cheese, eggs, coffee, meat, and canned goods. Labor and transportation shortages made it hard to harvest and move fruits and vegetables to market. As an alternative, the government encouraged its citizens to plant "Victory Gardens." They wanted individuals to provide their own fruits and vegetables in amounts that could sustain both their immediate families and nearby neighbors. Various methods of food preservation were encouraged; in fact, the sale of pressure cookers rose 377% in one year. The idea of gardening was patriotic. What a concept!

During that time, it was estimated that 20 million Victory Gardens were planted with enough produce grown across the country to produce 10 million tons of fruits and vegetables, equivalent to 40% of the national production. Wow!

You too can plant a modern-day version of a Victory Garden. You can plant nourishing gardens. You can plant gardens that are good for your soul. You can grow good memories. You can grow good food. You can grow healthy kids. And, through a garden, you can entice your kids to love fruits and vegetables and prefer them over other foods. You can plant seeds to healthier, more nourishing lives. Go out and savor the sunshine with your family.

Add Gardening to Your Recipe:

What are some reasons you want to plant a garden with your family?

What surprises you about the research on gardening?

What can you do today to start to bring your garden to life?

CHAPTER 5

GARDENING WITH YOUR FAMILY

Why try to explain miracles to your kids when you can just have them plant a garden. ~Robert Brault

As a young mom, I couldn't wait to plant my kids in the soil as soon as they could walk and hold a plastic shovel. While my kids were excited to put on their rain boots and dig into the soil, I was excited to take them to the garden with hopes of creating memories of planting the prettiest vegetable garden they ever did see. So with their rain boots on and their little set of shovels and rakes, it was time to dig in. We walked out to the garden and before I had given them instructions...the digging began.

Wait a minute—I wasn't ready for them to start digging yet! I hadn't told them what to do, where to dig, or how this was going to work!

Such is the life of family gardening. Sometimes you have to take a deep breath of patience in and release an exhale of perfection out, then repeat three or four times, letting it go as you remember that gardening is not about perfection, it's about creating memories and connection. Connections are created by using praise and encouragement to ensure the kids want to come back again. Criticism or negativity can seed discouragement, and your kids might not ever return to the garden.

So after I took those deep breaths, we planted peas, potatoes, tomatoes, and peppers. They dug the holes, put in the seeds, and shored up the seedlings in the soil. We all worked together to plant our very first family garden.

Now, maintaining the connection doesn't mean you can't provide direction. For example, try drawing a line in the soil to show where the peas could be planted, or trace an "X" where the potato hole needs to be dug. With just a little encouragement your kids will be eager to help. Keep in mind that planting both seeds and seedlings is essential because standing back and looking at the garden doesn't really look like much when the seeds are covered up by the soil!

It's helpful to keep expectations in check during the family gardening experience. Here are some simple ideas you can use to create nourishing moments together in the garden while creating a legacy of memories that will live for a lifetime.

Garden everywhere and anywhere. There's no right or wrong location for your family garden. The spot you choose is only limited by your imagination. Whether it's on a balcony with containers or in the backyard dug into the ground, it doesn't matter. It's about the memories, not about the perfect location.

Plant, harvest, repeat. Gardening year after year has the most influence on your family's connections and health. If you don't think you have the time, consider that several studies have indicated just spending an hour in the garden over a few weeks of time can make a positive difference in both eating habits and even blood pressure!

Talk about what it means to be nourished while gardening. Don't worry about creating lessons to teach in the garden, just do what comes naturally! That means talking about what plants need to live and how that relates to what we, as humans, need to live. I've included some garden conversation starters in the appendix.

Think young and younger. There is no wrong age to begin gardening with your kids. In one study, researchers looked at three to five year olds who were part of a preschool program over the course of 28 weeks where each week they focused on a fruit or vegetable in the garden. They noted a significant increase in kids asking for fruits and vegetables at meal and snack times. There was also a willingness to try and taste these fruits and vegetables with families reporting significant changes in attitudes about fruits and vegetables.[1]

Taste those fruits and vegetables. Introducing a dark green leafy vegetable to my six year old daughter was like asking her to eat a bug. She preferred sweet tasting foods over all things green. One day, however, I made quesadillas and tore up chard to put inside. She grew the chard herself and had weeded the entire area where it grew. Somehow putting the chard in the quesadilla made it more appealing. I was amazed at her new-found sense of adventure. In any other situation, if I had served my daughter a leaf of Swiss chard, she never would have eaten it.

Exploring fruits and vegetables through gardening is the perfect invitation to taste. Let your senses be your guide. Invite kids to explore vegetables by talking about their characteristics using senses of seeing, touching, smelling, hearing, and finally tasting. You will be amazed at the results.

It is important to keep the gardening experience positive as different kids experiment to find their favorites. There's a phrase we used in our garden classes to nurture a positive atmosphere for tasting, *"Don't yuck someone else's yum."* This phrase works well, teaching kids to learn how to be polite in their tastings. When we used this in the gardening classes, kids were actually saying it to each other if they caught someone *"yucking their yum."*

Come together around the table. The key here is instant gratification. Harvesting tomatoes in the afternoon that end up in a salad that evening makes for quick learning and appreciation. It's a true garden to table experience. Kids are excited to see something they have grown become part of the meal around the kitchen table.

Think of your garden as a legacy of love and health. What we sow we grow. Growing a garden together is more than the vegetables and fruits it provides. It's the legacy of love and health that is being created, cultivated, and sustained through the gardening process.

Gardening as They Grow

No matter what the age of your children, there are ways to get them involved and excited. Here are some tried-and-true ideas!

Less than five years old:

Make a digging garden. The garden is a natural learning space. It's where the kids can just come and dig into the ground. You may choose to plant something in that area that they can dig up at the end of the season, or you may choose to leave this little corner of the garden plant-free to give the kids some space to be creative, and well, to be kids!

Provide kid-sized tools. It's hard for small hands to manipulate adult-sized tools, so if you want your kids to feel at home in the garden, provide appropriately scaled garden gloves, kneelers, shovels, rakes, sun hats, and watering cans. These items can make great gifts for future gardeners at the end of the school year to kick start their summer.

Explore gardening books together. There are many children's books available that explain how different foods grow, how foods make it to the supermarket, and the power of nutrition. Make sure you find books with plenty of pictures for the preschool age. You can find a list in the appendix.

Tour greenhouses and plant nurseries. Look at the vegetable plants and notice their smells and colors. Talk about the fruits and vegetables that will develop from the seedlings you see. This can be a great learning experience which gets kids excited about the possibilities of planting their own gardens.

Elementary age:

Give your kids a choice. Ask them, *"What do you love to eat?"* Then, be sure to include ingredients from their favorite foods when you are planning the family garden. Maybe they will choose cucumbers that they can make into pickles, or they will want to grow tomatoes so they can make salsa. Of course, don't forget the strawberries they can turn into dessert. Any and all of these would be great options to start.

Design the garden together. Let your kids design the garden with the building and art tools they love to work with. They might choose paper and pencil, or they could choose Legos®. The minute I suggested to my son that we could design a garden using those little brightly colored bricks, he got to work. We were able to creatively see and feel how the garden would look that year.

Add some pizzazz to the garden. Let your kids help decorate the garden with kid-friendly solar sunflowers, or solar fireflies in jars. You can also ask your bigger kids to create garden markers by painting flat rocks or sticks using bright colors. Once dry, have them use permanent markers to write the corresponding names or draw pictures of the fruits or vegetables you have planted. These are all fun crafts that naturally engage kids in the gardening process and encourage them to return to the garden.

Visit a local nursery (the garden kind!). Take time to look at the seed packets to create a buzz about planting. The pictures and information contained on a seed packet can serve as a guide to figuring out what is to be planted in the garden. As a bonus, interpreting these planting guides often requires a bit of real life math story problems.

Play "Grow the Garden." This is just a fun way to do a little garden weeding, watering, or harvesting. Two or three times a week, find a 30 minute window of time to spend in the garden. Weed the garden by playing a game called "Plants and Robbers" where everyone grabs as many weeds as they can in five minutes. Use a watering can or hose to give the plants a drink. Check for any ripe and ready produce. Look for bugs and blooms. By investing just a few minutes several times a week and getting a bit creative, the garden tasks become more manageable.

Keep a garden journal. Journals provide a place for kids to follow the progress of the garden. They can measure how tall the plants have grown or chart other changes they notice. Don't forget to document what was harvested, even weighing your produce, and at the end of the season you will have a wonderful record of your garden accomplishments!

Have a garden patch picnic! Several times each summer, my children request to "go on a picnic." Kids don't care if a picnic is in their own backyard; it's the fun of eating outside and doing something different that is special. So, during the gardening season, celebrate the harvest by packing a garden patch picnic basket. The kids will love to get involved, and they can help plan the menu. Picnics can create memories to last a lifetime. Invite their friends too!

Middle school age and beyond:

Give the kids their own square of land. As a child, I had my own little corner of the garden where I was allowed to grow whatever I wanted, as long as it was within my little square. What did I grow? I was the herb grower of the family since the rest of the garden was devoted to vegetables. My garden felt valuable because the plants I grew enhanced everything else in the garden. Let your older kids cultivate their own corner of the garden. Let them choose how it will look, what it will grow, and how they take care of it.

Go online and learn together. Exploring websites, videos, and pictures of gardens can inspire a new way of thinking and doing.

Make harvesting fun. Play a family version of "Cropped!" the garden version of The Food Network's Chopped™ television show. Grab a basket and harvest what is ready to be picked from the garden. Bring it inside and create a new dish for the family meal that evening. You can compete basket-to-basket with the parents versus the kids, or siblings versus siblings. Invite the neighbors to judge. Whichever way you choose, keep it about the creativity and fun!

These are just a few ideas to get your family excited about gardening. Now it's time to brainstorm your family's gardening goals to help you determine your direction. Forget about complex plans, just keep your ideas simple enough to get the family growing. There's no need to dig up the entire back yard if you aren't ready to do that!

Measuring Success

Finally, decide how you will measure the success of your garden. Maybe a goal will be to grow one plant and make it last throughout the season without dying. Or maybe you would be thrilled when your kids actually tear into a pea pod and eat it without even bringing it into the house. Regardless of how you measure your accomplishments, gardening is a fun way to connect as a family and harvest healthy memories that will last a lifetime.

Determine your gardening goals:

What legacy do you want to leave as a mom?

How does a family garden fit into that legacy?

What's your hope for your garden?

What space do you have available now for a garden that receives six hours of sunlight each day?

Does that space have easy access to water?

What are your family's favorite recipes?

What foods can you grow as a family that will be related to the recipes your family loves?

What gardening outcome will you deem successful at the end of the season?

CHAPTER 6

A SACRED SPACE

Where you have a plot of land, however small, plant a garden. Staying close to the soil is good for the soul.
~Spencer W. Kimball

As you plan your garden, remember that you are creating a sacred space with your family, a space with a holy purpose. This space will allow for quiet reflection, renewal, and discovery during times of planting, weeding, and harvesting. The space you prepare will not only feed your family, but it will also become a space that will feed your soul. Creativity will incubate there and so will connection, to each other and to the earth. In its purest form, you are growing a garden of memories that will nourish your soul.

So how do you go about preparing and nurturing this holy space for your family? I suggest using a simple garden timeline to keep you on track so you can get started and not feel overwhelmed.

Winter—Reflection

There's just something about January that makes me want to get my life in order. I scramble to find every recipe my family likes to eat, organize them, and put them into a monthly rotation. I clean out closets, and I organize my thoughts and ideas.

Winter also happens to be when I think about our family garden. I think about the space, what will grow there, and how our family can connect together over this seemingly simple activity. Whether you have your garden already established, or you are planning to build the garden in the spring, the relative calm and coziness of winter provides a natural time for reflection and planning.

Are you still not sure where to begin? Here are a few topics to consider in the winter:

- Determine the size of your garden space.
- Determine the type of garden you wish to have (container, raised bed, or in-ground).
- Imagine what you want your space to look like. Visualize your sacred space by collecting pictures from magazines or pinning images to a gardening board on Pinterest.
- Include family members in the garden planning process, maybe talking to them over dinner one evening. Begin by asking what each member of your family loves to eat (even if you think you know already), then discuss the ingredients of those recipes that they can grow in the garden.

Spring—Planting

It's time to get growing! While winter is the reflective and planning stage, spring is the "doing" stage. There is something exhilarating about spring air; it is easy to get drawn into the vibrant signs of life and growth.

Tasks you and your family can do in the spring to focus on the garden include:

- Building your chosen style of garden
- Modifying the soil and space to freshen things up from winter if your garden already exists.
- Creating a list of all the fruits and vegetables the family is interested in planting.
- Designing the garden layout using graphing paper, then plotting and planning where the plants will grow.
- Sketching out a planting timeline so you know when your plants should go into the ground.
- Visiting your local garden nurseries to pick up either seeds or seedlings for planting.
- Gathering what you need for your family's gardening supplies.
- Starting seeds indoors that need a head start and preparing them for transplanting.

Summer—Savor

With its warm breezes and bright sunshine, summer is the time to savor the garden. There's something miraculous about a seed that sprouts into a beautiful plant that also produces food for our families.

The garden tasks of summer include:

- Watering deeply and weekly (unless you are container gardening, then daily watering may be needed in hot weather).
- Weeding together. Removing weeds might become the new conversation starter, comparing it to removing weeds of our lives.
- Harvesting what you so carefully planted as a family and bringing it into the kitchen.
- Dining with those who nourish you most, both with the plants and your family. Eating in the garden or next to it.

Finally, remember how important it is to teach your children to savor every moment, even when it feels like "work." Savor the weeding since it gives you time to be one with the earth. Savor the watering, remembering that each of us needs to be sprinkled with life-giving water on a regular basis. Savor the harvesting, recalling what went into getting the plants to grow, thrive, and produce food for our families.

Fall—Legacy

Fall is the final stop in the cycle of the garden, and it's all about cultivating a legacy of learning together, of connecting together, and of enjoying the harvest with each other.

Fall chores include:

- Pulling out remaining vines and plants and putting them into your compost bin.
- Removing any weeds.
- Tilling the garden to create a smooth surface in preparation for next spring.
- Hosting a harvest dinner for your neighbors, friends, and family. This is an opportunity to share in the harvest, exchange recipes, and even preserve the abundance.
- Taking some time to celebrate your gardening challenges and wins, to document the things you and your family learned, and to record what you wish to try next year. Even the youngest children can help create a garden scrapbook with of photos of your harvest!

I hope that you find that by using this simple timeline, a family garden seems more doable. You will be surprised at how fast the growing season passes and you will wish for it to extend.

Your Sacred Space

I want you to now visualize the space and style of your garden—your sacred space and the site of future memories and nourishment.

I invite you to go outside and stand in your yard, wherever you see your family garden being planted. It may be in your front yard, or it may be in the back yard. It may be that you have no yard, but you have a patio or deck on which you can set containers. It may be you wish to plant a raised bed style garden. Wherever you choose to plant this garden, the best way to determine if the space will work is to physically go stand there. Stand there when it's sunny, and stand there when it is shady. Take a good look around.

Identify Your Water Source

First and foremost, nothing grows without water. Water is the key ingredient to getting seeds to sprout, to getting a plant to produce fruit, and to protecting the plants in the summer's heat. Not only is it important for our gardens to have water, it's also true for ourselves. The water we drink sustains us and gets us through the day. While you may think of actual water here, there's actually something greater. It's the water that's found in our faith and spirituality. How we water our faith makes a tremendous difference in our life.

Take a moment to think of a plant that is stressed from lack of water. It droops, developing smaller than normal leaves, the remaining leaves have edges that turn brown, and the fruit produced by the plant is smaller than you would expect.

Isn't that true for us as well? When we choose not to drink up faith in something bigger than us, it stresses us too. This stress can show up in a droopy stance which compromises our confidence. It can also show up as "rough edges" in us—anxiety, depression, a sharp tongue, etc.

Unless we drink daily from the water of faith, the quality of our work and relationships will weaken and become unstable. Just as dramatic fluctuations in moisture can cause harm to plants, a lack of spiritual connection will cause the growth and quality of our "fruits and vegetables" to suffer as well. We must evenly and consistently water our plants and ourselves to be the best we can be.

As a hospital dietitian it was often hard for me to separate what was happening to a patient from my own fears. I had fears of dying before I was 30, of dying before my kids were grown, and of leaving my husband to raise them on his own. Although this fear lived in my head for a while, it eventually started to cause physical symptoms like heart palpitations and several visits to the emergency room. On one such occasion, my friend from work walked me to the ER because I refused a wheelchair. My need to control was still strong despite my fear! Another time, I was placed in a critical care bed next to someone who was literally having a heart attack. If that doesn't intensify panic, I don't know what will.

After this experience, I met with a doctor who gave me some great advice. *When my daily life feels out of control, I can start my day with the One who is in control and put my trust there.*

The battle is ongoing, but I do believe that's when I started experiencing some pretty radical life changes. A Christian radio station found me—I assure you, I wasn't looking for it—and I began listening. I believe that the words I heard through the radio were meant to be spoken to me. At a time when I felt like I was living "in" my head, listening to these spiritual messages got me "out" of my head. That radio station was my water...and I needed it daily.

There are a few things we can do to prevent both our plants and ourselves from drying out and suffering the "lack" that leads to stress. To prevent plants from drying out too quickly, you can add mulch. Mulch is a layer of straw, grass clippings, leaves, or bark that is added to the top of the soil around the plants to help retain moisture in the soil underneath. It prevents the wind from drying out the soil because it acts as a blanket. We too can surround ourselves with a blanket of uplifting words, uplifting music, uplifting people, and uplifting spaces to protect us from our stress.

Hot summer days are the most stressful to a plant because without adequate water, drying winds and hot temperatures will cause plants to wilt. To counteract this, we must water deeply, directly onto the roots, first thing in the morning. Watering in the morning allows the garden to have the day to absorb the moisture, while watering the roots encourages them to spread deep into the soil. Watering in the morning, rather than overnight, also prevents excess moisture from lingering on leaves, stems, and fruit which can lead to disease and fungus growth on the fragile plants.

It is also best for us to water ourselves and our souls in the morning—to get up a little earlier than the rest of our family, taking some quiet time to rejuvenate. Reading inspiring words, listening to positive and encouraging music, starting the day in gratitude, and journaling can help us to withstand the most stressful times in our lives.

Of course, to be able to water the garden when it needs rejuvenation, the water source needs to be close to the garden space. Easy access is essential to keep consistent moisture levels. This parallels our needs as well. When we keep our rejuvenating sources close to us, we will use them more consistently.

Sunshine, the Light of Life

All nourishing gardens need sun. Specifically, vegetable gardens need at least six hours of sunlight per day. Plants derive their energy from sunlight. That fancy word, photosynthesis, comes into play here. The more light, the greater food production of the plant. If sunlight is lacking, the plant will not produce what it is capable of, and it will ultimately die. The warmth and light provided by the sun is needed for the plant to convert the soil nutrients into nourishment for us.

The sun nourishes us as well. It's where we receive the sunshine vitamin, Vitamin D, which is essential to so many processes in our body. While plants require a bit more than we do, our need for sunshine is the same. Fresh air, clearer thinking, and being able to move our bodies contributes to our own ability to create a nourishing life.

Nourishing Soil Nourishes Us

Another assessment to make as we visualize the sacred space is to determine the state of our soil. Soil provides fuel for the plant to grow and sustain itself to produce food. The soil base provides the roots with a matrix in which to anchor themselves, delivering water and nutrients to the plants so they can produce food that is in turn healthy for us.

The garden soil must be loose and fluffy, not hard and compacted. Compacted soil makes it hard to have healthy plants. When seeds emerge from the ground, the plants want to stretch and grow. Compacted soil restricts this ability, making it harder for plant roots to spread out. This compaction limits access to soil nutrients and moisture and can weaken the plant's ability to stabilize itself in the ground.

In addition, all plants need nutrients. Plants need balanced amounts of nitrogen, phosphorus, and potassium. Nitrogen contributes to plant growth, lush leaves and stems, and dark green foliage. Phosphorus is important for strong roots, flowers, fruits, and seeds. Potassium is vital for stress proofing plants and for the production of fruits and vegetables.

We need these nutrients as well. Nutrients from these plants protect our bodies from stress and disease, and nutrients are necessary for growing and producing.

How do you know if your soil is a healthy and nourishing space where plants will thrive and grow? You complete a soil test. A soil test provides knowledge of what our soil is like and whether it can sustain life. To get an idea of the structure of your soil, or what it is made of, take a soil sample with a small shovel from three to five locations in your garden. Stir those samples together in a pail and take a look at the soil you've mixed. Your soil should look dark, like crumbles of chocolate cake. It should feel loose and spongy and smell earthy and rich. If your soil is gritty and falls apart readily in your hands, your soil is too sandy. If your soil is sticky and balls up easily, it's heavy in clay. What you need is a mixture of the two, and that can be accomplished by adding compost.

To get a detailed analysis of the nutrients in your soil, which I recommend you do yearly, take the sample to your local soil management office where you will get an in-depth look at the nutrients in your soil. Specific instructions to correct nutrient deficiencies will accompany these reports and can help you to optimize the growing conditions so your plants can thrive.

At the start of each growing season, wise gardeners will add compost to their gardens. You can make your own if you wish, or purchase compost, like yard and waste compost, composted manure, mushroom compost, and vermicompost (from earthworms).

To make your own compost, I highly suggest the reference on the University of Minnesota Yard and Garden website, entitled *Backyard Composting*. There are a few steps you should take to ensure a high nutrient dense compost including choosing the right ingredients to be composted. Examples include shrub clippings, faded flowers, leftover plants, leaves, straw, coffee grounds, eggshells, fruit and vegetable scraps, shredded newspaper (black and white print), small amounts of wood ash, and sawdust. In addition to these, soil and a nitrogen source need to be added. Check out the resource I suggested for full details.

Soil Tests and Soul Tests

Garden soil can take a beating. It can become compacted or become depleted of nutrients. We can also become "compacted," limiting ourselves when we try to maintain a tightly scheduled life. We don't grow in the areas we need to grow in. We don't live guided by our purpose, and we don't produce and harvest all we can to become the best we can be. We need to loosen up our schedules and provide ourselves and our families with the "nutrients" we need to survive life's stressors, helping us endure those times when we aren't consuming enough life-giving water or we miss out on the essential ingredients.

So we have soil tests for our garden. What about soul tests for our lives? Ask yourself, what do you want to grow in your life? How will you create a more intentional life, a life that produces abundantly in the form of balance and purpose? What will you prune away to enhance your growth? Maybe it's time to apply the lifestyle compost recipe from Chapter 3 to nourish your life.

The Highs and Lows of Garden Types

Now that you have dug into the soil and assessed its vitality, what type of garden will house that soil? Whether you choose a traditional in-ground garden, experiment with a raised bed garden, or you are growing close to the house in container gardens, it is important to do what works well in your space.

In-ground gardens. An in-ground garden has one major advantage—space. Often found in backyards, in-ground gardens require digging up the grass, removing it, and then tilling up the soil underneath. If you have a large yard space, an in-ground garden can be a good fit. Even if you have a small yard, an in-ground garden can work. This type of garden is for anyone really. If your yard is flat, without slopes, this style is great. Soil health is a priority in this garden, since you will be digging the vegetables and fruits right into the ground. The appendix has a step-by-step outline of how to dig out an in-ground garden.

Raised bed gardens. Do you have bad soil? A slope in your yard? I have both of these problems in our current yard. That's why I switched to a raised bed garden several years ago. It was a simple way to optimize our space. It even works if you have a yard of concrete or pavement.

Raised beds have better soil structure and drainage, allowing the soil to warm up sooner than an in-ground garden. Raised bed gardens also bring the plants up to a comfortable working level. The other thing I love about raised beds is that there isn't a lot of walking on the soil as in an in-ground garden which can contribute to a hard, compacted soil environment.

Consider whether you can reach from one side or both sides of your raised bed garden. If you place the beds so you can only reach from one side of the space, the beds should be a maximum of 30 inches wide. If you can access the bed from both sides, then the garden beds could be up to five feet wide.

Designing the raised bed garden is simple. You can opt for a four foot-by-four foot square, a four-by-eight foot rectangle or even an L-shaped garden as you start your gardening journey. The height of the garden frame can be six inches to two feet, or even higher if you prefer to stand and garden as a family.

The bed frames themselves are made mostly of wood, but also can be made of stone pavers. To create a sturdy frame for the raised bed garden, choose untreated, rot-resistant lumber like cedar. Do not use railroad ties because they contain toxins. Treated lumber is also not recommended due to the potential of arsenic leaching out of the wood and into the soil where plants can absorb it.

Once the frame is built, fill the garden to within inches of the top with equal parts top soil and compost. The soil will settle throughout the season. And just like we need to add a little compost to our lives now and then, be sure to add two to four inches of compost each year when you are preparing your gardens.

Container gardens. Maybe you are lacking physical space in your yard for a garden, or you do not have a yard at all. Or maybe you just want to try gardening on a smaller scale to see how it goes before you dig into the lawn. No matter what your reason, container gardening is an easy way to grow vegetables just steps from your door. All that is required is a sunny, open area with plenty of air circulation.

To give plants a healthy start, use clean containers with drainage holes. Be sure the containers are large enough to accommodate the mature size of the plant you intend to grow. You will probably need more space than you expect for larger plants. Containers that are 10 inches wide and 12 inches deep will accommodate most vegetable plants, but tomatoes will require larger containers. If you need to drill drainage holes, use a ¼ inch drill bit to make several holes on the bottom of the container. If you need to provide support for a large plant, it's easy to add a cage over your growing tomato plants or a trellis for your cucumbers. Keep in mind the container itself should be sturdy enough to withstand the additional weight of the vining plants.

Whether you have a patio, deck, balcony, or front porch, the goal with this type of gardening is finding the spot that receives a minimum of six hours of sunlight per day. Northern climate container gardeners will benefit from a southern exposure and southern climate gardeners need to be alert for the excess heat generated by pavement or cement. There is no need to cook your vegetables before they are ready to be cooked in your kitchen!

Watering is key when you use containers because they quickly dry out in heat or in windy conditions. The type of container you use can also make a difference in your watering schedule. For example, terra-cotta planters are porous and dry out more quickly, and dark colored planters absorb sunlight making the soil increase in temperature.

It is important to use a soil mix created specifically for container gardening. You can buy this type of soil at your local nursery or gardening store, or you can make your own growing soil by mixing equal parts peat moss, potting soil, and vermiculite or perlite. Alternatively, you can mix equal parts garden soil and compost. Fill your containers to within an inch or two of the rim.

Plant your container garden when you would normally plant any garden. You can plant seeds directly into the container or transplant seedlings into the soil. Water the soil thoroughly before you plant, allowing the moisture to distribute throughout the soil mixture. After planting, keep the soil in the container garden from drying out by watering frequently and using a gentle sprinkle.

At the end of the season, wash the containers thoroughly to prevent the spread of disease and/or pests that might have found their way into the soil. Rinse the containers with a solution of one part bleach to 10 parts water, then rinse with clean water and store in a dry area.

Your Sacred Space

One summer, we arrived home after baseball practice and the first thing I heard was, *"Let's go check the garden!"* That was truly music to my ears. Watching my children run from the car to the garden to discover the first ripe strawberry was pure excitement and joy. It was then I realized this garden of ours was a sacred space. A space with a holy purpose. A space to grow fruits and vegetables and to grow good eaters. A space to grow more connected as a family.

This book contains a lot of information about gardens, but I don't want you to feel overwhelmed. There is no need for perfection in gardening; in fact, with just a little care, a garden can be a very forgiving place.

Learning about gardening will be a series of trial and error experiences, just like life is a series of trial and error experiences. We test the soil to determine what needs to be added or what is missing. We apply compost to improve the soil. We test our souls to determine what needs to be added or what needs to be pruned away, and we follow the compost recipe. Life isn't about perfection, it's about heading in the direction to where we set our intentions we hold and the hope to create a life that is nourishing.

Create the recipe to a nourishing life:
How do you see your garden as a sacred space, one that has a holy purpose?

What do you want the garden to do for you and your family?

Which fruits and vegetables do you intend to grow?

Visualize your garden space, assess the water, sunlight and soil needs of your garden.

On some blank graphing paper, sketch your family garden.

CHAPTER 7

THE NOURISHING PLANTS

Everything that slows us down and forces patience,
everything that sets us back into the slow circles of nature,
is a help. Gardening is an instrument of grace.
~May Sarton

Sowing a seed in soil takes patience. Patience to watch for the first leaf to sprout, patience to transplant that seedling into the garden, and patience to allow the fruit to finally develop. You've reached the chapter of sowing and growing—sowing seeds and growing seedlings into plants so we can harvest what we have planted. Every time we eat is an opportunity to nourish ourselves. So, with every fruit or vegetable you see in this chapter, you will get a sense of why you might plant them in your garden, why they are so nourishing to us, and why they belong on our tables.

You will also find ideas for the best varieties to plant based on northern climate recommendations, since these areas have the shortest growing seasons. Southern climates can use these varieties as well, adjusting for seasonality. I've also included some instructions about how to plant each fruit and vegetable and when to harvest.

Be intentional. Make purposeful choices about what you will plant. Maybe your choices will be based around a recipe your family loves in the summer. It could be because you want enough produce to share or give to others. Whatever the reason, give some thought as to why you want to grow that certain vegetable or fruit:

- Taste and flavor
- Ease of growing
- Produces a lot (high yield)
- Easy to make into a favorite recipe
- Nutritious
- Easy to store or it lasts a while
- Fun to grow or to try something new

Identifying what is important to you and your family will make choosing plants easier. Maybe you want to focus on growing vegetables for salsa or fruits and vegetables for smoothies. Maybe you want to plant lettuce in the spring so you can harvest it throughout the summer for salads every day. Maybe you want to focus on eating for a healthy heart, so you choose to grow foods that are high in potassium. Whatever the reason(s), identifying them will help you clarify what you hope to grow, and rather than finding your kids using the Brussels sprout stalk as a baseball bat (yes, that actually happened!), you will actually find them eating them!

With a garden that receives full sun and is easily accessible with good soil, your planting options are endless. Feel free to start small if this is your first time. Try four or five different vegetables in your first family garden to prevent feeling overwhelmed. There's power in starting small.

Starting Seeds Indoors or Out

Some vegetables require direct seeding, which means sowing the seeds directly into the ground you intend to harvest them from. Other vegetables do better if you start the seed inside and transplant the seedlings outside. Indoor seeding allows for the planting of longer season vegetables that might not otherwise reach harvest prior to the first fall frost in your specific plant hardiness zone. You can find out the frost dates in your area by contacting the local extension service in your state so you know when it is safe to plant outside.

Starting seeds indoors requires the same attention to light, moisture, and soil as planting outdoors. In fact, many seedlings are lost due to insufficient light indoors. Southern facing windows are best, or you can make your own growing light by using a fluorescent light source with one warm white bulb and one cool white bulb. The best soil for starting seeds is a soil-less or peat-lite mix since actual garden soil contains organisms that can damage young plants, and it doesn't drain well.

All kinds of containers can be used to start seeds, including flats, pots, clean cans, cut-off milk cartons, small food tubs, and egg cartons. Just be sure they are clean and have good drainage by using a nail to punch holes into the bottom of each container. An easy way to do this is to hold a nail with a pliers and warm the end of a nail with the flame of a candle, slowly pushing the nail through the container. Then, fill the containers to two-thirds with moist, soil-less or peat-lite mix. For larger seeds, sow one or two seeds per space directly into the container. Sow smaller seeds on the surface of the soil. Follow the package directions and you will be good to grow!

The best way to water newly planted seeds is by misting since the light spray won't wash out and displace the seeds that were planted. It may be beneficial to cover the container with plastic wrap to keep moisture inside especially when winter air is drier. Set the containers away from sunlight in a location between 60 to 75 degrees. Once the seeds have germinated, remove the plastic wrap and place seeds in the light. Keep the soil moist but not so damp that fungus forms and kills the seedling. Once the seedlings develop two true leaves, thin the plants to one per pot.

When directly seeding into garden soil, the general rule is planting seeds to a depth of 4 to 5 times the side width of the seed. In some cases, the seeds are very tiny which means the planting depth will be quite shallow. In other cases, the seeds will be quite large, such as bean seeds, and they will be planted slightly deeper into the soil.

Planting at the right depth is important since planting too shallow can make the seed susceptible to extreme drying, poor root development, and poor plant stature. On the other hand, planting too deep may result in poor or delayed emergence of the seedling. Refer to the planting directions on the seed packages for more specifics.

Directly seeding into the garden is quite simple. Just prepare a furrow or channel in the soil to the desired planting depth. Evenly distribute the seed according to package directions and firm up (don't compact) the soil over the furrow after planting. Water lightly yet thoroughly. This type of planting is called "row-cropping" since we are planting seeds in single file lines with room to walk between the rows. Weeding this type of garden will be slightly easier since you will be able to get in and out of the rows with tools like a hoe. The flip side of this is that less fruits and vegetables are produced in your garden since more space is left open for walking.

Another method, called intensive planting, is a technique of planting vegetables to maximize growing space. Instead of one straight row, you broadcast seeds over a swath of soil, often one to four feet wide. Those seeds grow in close proximity to one another, helping to reduce weeds while keeping the soil cooler. Harvesting is faster since the fruits and vegetables are so close together. Hand weeding will be a must, however, since tools will not likely fit between plants. Intensive planting is a quick and easy way to get your garden growing.

You may also have heard of square foot gardening, which is a style of intensive planting. This is where you divide the garden into smaller beds, four feet by four feet, then you divide them even further into one foot square sections, where each square is then planted with one, four, nine, or sixteen plants depending on the type of plant and space it requires. Refer to the website, www.gardeners.com, for guidelines on the number of plants you can sow per square foot. This is based on the type of vegetable.

I've tried both methods of planting and honestly, I prefer planting in rows because it appears neat and organized, and my kids and I are able to get between the rows to remove weeds. Try both and see which your family prefers!

Transplanting a seedling into the garden allows us to grow some longer season vegetables in a shorter amount of time since the seed has been previously started. To transplant a seedling, whether it's from your own indoor growing or purchased from a garden nursery, the process is the same. The primary concern is avoiding transplant shock. This happens when a plant, once protected from harsh weather, is now exposed to the elements. Our job is to acclimate the seedling prior to planting it into the garden soil. To do this it's wise to withhold water slightly to help the plants adapt to the moisture fluctuations that are true to nature. You can also set the plant outdoors during the day, then bring it back in again at night for three or four days prior to planting outside.

On planting day, it's best to transplant in the evening or on a cloudy, calm day. Dig a hole just large enough to fit the roots of the plant, slightly deeper than the container itself. Plant the seedling, firming the soil around the stem.

I've also included companion plants with each fruit or vegetable. These companions are like friends; they grow well together and reduce pests and disease by being planted together. You will also notice that what grows together in the garden often goes well together in the kitchen. Think of the recipe combinations!

To Nourish

One of the main reasons people plant gardens is to provide a ready source of nutritious fruits and vegetables for their families to eat. Quick and easy access to these nourishing foods make it much simpler to cook and eat the food that can sustain a healthy lifestyle.

How do we know which foods are the most nourishing? Which foods would be best for blood pressure? Which foods help us fight inflammation, and which foods are beneficial for our digestive systems? With each vegetable or fruit listed, I've included a section, "To Nourish," showing you the ways that food will nourish you. These fruits and vegetables provide essential nutrients needed to live a nourishing life. I encourage you to grow the foods you need to harvest the health you desire.

One thing you will note as you read about these plants is that many of the garden vegetables and fruits are anti-inflammatory foods. These foods work to fight and repair damage cells. Damaged cells are inflamed, putting us at higher risk for diseases like cancer, heart disease, and diabetes.

Now, it's time to dream. As you go through the following pages of fruits and vegetables, make note of what interests you, and whether you would like to plant it in your family garden. Your choices will depend on the space you have and what your family will eat. Growing fruits and vegetables that your family loves to eat will coax them to visit to the garden more frequently.

Arugula

To Nourish	Anti-inflammation
In the Kitchen	Peppery flavor. Popular in pesto and salads, paninis, and pasta.
To Plant	Cool season vegetable. Plant seeds 3 to 4 inches apart, directly into the garden.
To Harvest	Pick outer leaves for longer harvest time; younger leaves are more tender.
Companions	Tomatoes, spinach, basil, red cabbage, strawberries
Varieties to Grow	Roquette, Runway, Garden

Broccoli

To Nourish	Healthy digestion, anti-inflammation
In the Kitchen	Stir-fry, pasta, salads, steam, grate stalks into slaw, add to soups, use as baked potato topping or pizza topping, dip florets with salsa or hummus.
To Plant	Cool season vegetable. Start seeds indoors. Transplant seedlings, 18 inches apart, into the garden.
To Harvest	Harvest full heads before flowers develop. Cut stalk to harvest, harvest side shoots as they form.
Companions	Peas, scallions, carrots, lettuce
Varieties to Grow	Munchkin, Early Dividend, Bonanza, Packman, Premium Crop, Arcadia, Captain, Patriot

Beans

To Nourish	Anti- inflammation, healthy digestion, heart health
In the Kitchen	Crunchy texture. Eat raw or steam, add into casseroles, soups, salads, and stir-fry.
To Plant	Warm season vegetable. Plant seeds, 8 inches apart, directly into garden.
To Harvest	Pick every other day when beans begin to elongate.
Companions	Basil, yellow squash, eggplant, tomatoes
Varieties to Grow	**Dry:** French Horticultural, Great Northern, Jacob's Cattle, Soldier, Mung, Navy, Pinto, Red Kidney **Bush Green Bean:** Straight N' Narrow, Provider, Romano, Green Ruler, Green Crop, Jade, Strike, Tavera, Derby, Romanette, Bush Blue Lake 274, Mon Petit Cheri **Lima:** Henderson, Jackson Wonder **Bush Purple:** Royal Burgundy, Purple Queen **Bush Yellow:** Roc D'or, Dorabel, Goldcrop, Rocquencourt, Goldkist, Wax Romano, Dragon's Tongue **Pole:** Early Riser, Northeaster, Kentucky Blue Lake, Kentucky Wonder, Liana

Beets

To Nourish	Anti-inflammation
In the Kitchen	Roast, slice, add to salads.
To Plant	Cool season vegetable. Plant seeds, 3 to 4 inches apart, directly into garden.
To Harvest	Pull beets from ground when they are young and more tender, approximately 2 inches in diameter—greens are edible too.
Companions	Cabbage, kale, mustard, greens, spinach
Varieties to Grow	**Globe:** Ruby Queen, Red Ace, Pacemaker II **Cylindra:** Formanova, Cylindra

Brussels Sprouts

To Nourish	Anti-inflammation, healthy digestion
In the Kitchen	Dust with brown sugar and a pinch of salt, microwave five minutes. Roast at 400ºF for 40 minutes. Drizzle with Italian dressing and grill. Add to stir-fry.
To Plant	Cool season vegetable. Start seeds indoors. Transplant seedlings, 18 to 24 inches apart, directly into garden.
To Harvest	Pick individual sprouts from the bottom up, picking when sprout is 1 to 2 inches in diameter. Sprouts sweeten after a hard frost.
Companions	Acorn squash, tomatoes, onions, potatoes
Varieties to Grow	Masterline, Prince Marvel, Jade Cross

Cabbage

To Nourish	Anti-inflammation, healthy digestion
In the Kitchen	Stir-fry, add to salads, use as topping for fish tacos.
To Plant	Start seeds indoors. Transplant seedlings, 18 to 48 inches apart, directly into garden.
To Harvest	Cut head from base of plant when head feels solid and firm.
Companions	Onions, potatoes, carrots, tomatoes
Varieties to Grow	**Chinese:** Blues, Kasumi **Green:** Polar Green, Early Jersey Wakefield, Dynamo, Stonehead, Market Topper, Green Boy, Stonehold, Copenheaven, Discovery, Fortuna **Red:** Salad Delight, Red Dynastyv, Meteorv, Red Express

Cantaloupe

To Nourish	Anti-inflammation, heart health
In the Kitchen	Fruit kebobs, melon salsa, sweet salads, eat raw or freeze chunks and eat frozen.
To Plant	Start seeds indoors. Transplant seedlings, 36-42 inches apart, directly into garden.
To Harvest	Pick when rind color shifts from gray-green to yellowish. Ripe melons slip easily from the vine.
Companions	Strawberries, watermelon, basil, mint
Varieties to Grow	Earlisweet, Earligold, Earliqueen, Fastbreak, French Orange, Rocky Sweet, Touchdown, Burpee Hybrid, Superstar, Athena

Carrots

To Nourish	Anti-inflammation, healthy digestion, heart health
In the Kitchen	Smoothies, eat raw, stir-fry, grate into salads, roast, or sauté.
To Plant	Plant seeds, 2 to 4 inches apart, directly into garden.
To Harvest	Harvest when desired size is achieved.
Companions	Beets, green peas, potatoes, dill
Varieties to Grow	Nanco, Touchon, Scarlet Nantes, A Plus, Chantenay, Sweet Sunshine, Bolero, Nutra-Red, Apache, Vita Sweet 781

Cauliflower

To Nourish	Anti-inflammation
In the Kitchen	Stir-fry, soup, steam and mash, use as a pizza crust, roast, add to salads.
To Plant	Start seeds indoors. Transplant seedlings, 18 inches apart, directly into garden.
To Harvest	Pick when heads are fully formed and buds are tight; cut main stem just below head.
Companions	Broccoli, carrots, green peas, spinach
Varieties to Grow	Silver Cup, Snow Crown, Purplehead, Fremont, Andes, White Sales, Candid Charm, Violet Queen, Stardust

Celery

To Nourish	Anti-inflammation, healthy digestion
In the Kitchen	Salads, stews, stir-fry, soups, juices, or slice and eat raw.
To Plant	Cool season vegetable. Start seeds indoors. Transplant seedlings, 8 inches apart, directly into garden.
To Harvest	Once celery reaches desired size, pull individual stalks from bunches as needed or cut whole heads of celery at the soil line.
Companions	Carrots, potatoes, onions, leaf lettuce
Varieties to Grow	Tango

Corn

To Nourish	Anti-inflammation, healthy digestion
In the Kitchen	Soup, guacamole, salsa, salads, breads. Steam, grill or boil ears.
To Plant	Plant seeds, 8 to 12 inches apart, directly into garden.
To Harvest	Ready to harvest when silk is brown at top of corn ear and ears of corn feel plump and not skinny.
Companions	Tomatoes, lettuce, cucumbers, watermelon
Varieties to Grow	**Popping:** Pretty Pops, Lopop12 **Sugar Enhanced:** Seneca Arrowhead, Seneca Pronto, Quickie, Seneca Sensation, Temptation, Ambrosia, Bodacious, Mystique, Alpine, For Heaven's Sake, Delectable, Argent

Cucumbers

To Nourish	Anti-inflammation, healthy digestion
In the Kitchen	Add to salads, wraps, sandwiches.
To Plant	Start seeds indoors. Transplant seedlings, 36 to 60 inches apart depending on variety, directly into garden.
To Harvest	Pick when cucumbers reach desired size. Use shears to clip from vine or twist and pull gently.
Companions	Tomatoes, lettuce, dill, onions
Varieties to Grow	**Pickling:** Patio Pickle, Northern Pickling, Cool Breeze, Eureka, H-19 Arkansas Little Leaf, Liberty **Slicing:** Dasher II, Spacemaster, Victory, Marketmore 76, Sweet Slice, Fanfare, Marketmore 66

Eggplant

To Nourish	Anti-inflammation, healthy digestion
In the Kitchen	Use as meat substitute, ratatouille, eggplant lasagna, kebobs, pizza, roast, peel and toss with pasta. Slice rounds and dip into beaten egg whites, then into bread crumbs, sprinkle with Parmesan and bake until tender.
To Plant	Start seeds indoors. Transplant seedlings, 24 to 36 inches apart, directly into garden.
To Harvest	Pick when fruit skin becomes glossy, clipping fruit stem.
Companions	Tomatoes, basil, kale, hot peppers
Varieties to Grow	Cloud Nine, Green Goddess, Ichiban, Dusky, Burpee Hybrid, Vittoria, Ghostbuster

Honeydew

To Nourish	Anti-inflammation, heart health
In the Kitchen	Freeze cubes and make into freeze pops. Add fresh cubed to salads, or melon salsa, fruit kebobs, or cold soup.
To Plant	Start seeds indoors. Transplant seedlings, 36 to 42 inches apart, directly into garden.
To Harvest	Pick when rind color changes from cream to white. Ripe melons slip easily from the vine.
Plant Friends	Corn, pumpkin, radish, squash
Varieties to Grow	Earlidew, Honey-I-Dew

Kale

To Nourish	Anti-inflammation, bone health, heart health, healthy digestion
In the Kitchen	Toss into pasta, add to salad, stir-fry and substitute for spinach in any recipe, sauté with vegetables, add to soups.
To Plant	Cool season vegetable. Plant seeds, 12 to 24 inches apart, directly into garden.
To Harvest	Harvest leaves as soon as they are desirable size, picking outer leaves first.
Companions	Onions, mustard greens, beets
Varieties to Grow	Winterbor

Kohlrabi

To Nourish	Anti-inflammation, healthy digestion
In the Kitchen	Tastes like a mix of cucumber and broccoli, Eat raw, add to salad or cooked into soups, stews and stir-fry.
To Plant	Cool season vegetable. Plant seeds or seedlings, 9 to 12 inches apart, directly into garden.
To Harvest	Harvest when globes are 2.5 to 4 inches across in diameter. Cut stem from roots. Leaves are also edible.
Companions	Leaf lettuce, broccoli, scallions, cauliflower
Varieties to Grow	Kolibri, Grand Duke, Early White Vienna, Early Purple Vienna

Leek

To Nourish	Healthy digestion, anti-inflammation
In the Kitchen	Potato and leek soup, quiche, roast with other vegetables, add to soups and stews.
To Plant	Cool season vegetable. Start seeds indoors. Transplant seedlings, 6 inches apart, directly into garden.
To Harvest	Harvest at any size, using smaller leaks like scallions or wait for 1 inch diameter stems. Pull easily when soil is moist. In dry soil, use a digging fork. Wash well.
Companions	Potatoes, carrots, tomatoes, spinach
Varieties to Grow	Electra, Large American Flag

Lettuce

To Nourish	Anti-inflammation
In the Kitchen	Salad!
To Plant	Cool season vegetable. Plant seeds, 6 to 18 inches apart, directly into garden.
To Harvest	Pick leaves from outside in, or wait to harvest whole heads.
Companions	Tomatoes, scallions, arugula, strawberries
Varieties to Grow	**Butterhead:** Kagraner, Sommer, Buttercrunch, Tom Thumb **Head:** Mini-Green, Summertime, Burpee's Iceburg, Rosey **Romaine:** Little Gem, Romulus, Cosmo **Leaf:** Oakleaf, Grand Rapids, Black-Seeded Simpson, Red Sails, Lolla Rossa Atsina **Salad Greens:** Kyona/Mizuna, Tendergreens (Mustard), Green Cured Ruffec (Endive), Tatsoi

Onions

To Nourish	Anti-inflammation
In the Kitchen	Sauté, grill, roast, add to soups, stir-fry, pasta, salads.
To Plant	Plant sets (mini bulbs), 6 inches apart, directly into garden.
To Harvest	Harvest while small or wait until bulbs form. Harvest full-size onion bulbs when most leaves are bending over.
Companions	Cilantro, tomatoes, peppers, spinach
Varieties to Grow	Greek Salad, Superstar, Candy, Big Daddy, Big Mama, Sweet Spanish, Sweet Sandwich, Red Burgermaster, Yellow Sweet Spanish, Frontier, Stuttgarter

Parsnips

To Nourish	Anti-inflammation, healthy digestion
In the Kitchen	Roast, add to soups and stews.
To Plant	Plant seeds, 4 inches apart, directly into garden.
To Harvest	Dig roots at end of growing season, during winter or even better the following spring. To leave in over winter, cover with 10 inches of mulch.
Companions	Green peas, leeks, broccoli, summer squash
Varieties to Grow	All-American Hollow Crown, Harris' Model

Peas

To Nourish	Anti-inflammation, healthy digestion
In the Kitchen	Raw or cooked, brightens up any salad or soup, stews or casseroles. Stir into cooked rice. Mash and add to guacamole. Add to stir-fry or pasta.
To Plant	Cool season vegetable. Plant seeds, 5 inches apart, directly into garden.
To Harvest	Pick often and at the stage you desire, early for snow pea style, mid-plump to eat peas and the pod or wait for shell to fill overly plump for shelling only.
Companions	Leaf lettuce, broccoli, scallions, arugula
Varieties to Grow	**Snap (eat pod when plump):** Sugar Snap, Super Sugar Mel, Sugar Daddy **Garden (eat peas inside only):** Knight, Maestro, Sparkle, Green Arrow, Wando, Mr. Big **Snow (eat pod before peas swell):** Oregon Sugar Pod, Little Sweetie, Super Sugar Pod, Mammoth Melting Sugar

Peppers

To Nourish	Anti-inflammation, healthy digestion
In the Kitchen	Stuff, toss into stir-fry, soups or chili. Add to salads or sandwiches, grill or eat raw.
To Plant	Start seeds indoors. Transplant seedlings, 18 to 36 inches apart, directly into garden.
To Harvest	Use shears to cut peppers instead of pulling off plant.
Companions	Tomatoes, onions, cilantro, parsley
Varieties to Grow	**Ripens to yellow/brown:** Sweet Chocolate, Sunrise Orange, Golden Bell, Golden Calwonder **Ripens to Red:** Superset, Ace, Park's Early Thickset, Ma Belle, Gypsy, Northstar, Super Red Pimento, Lady Bell, Fat N' Sassy, Red Start, Crispy, Green Boy, Islander **Hot:** Thai Hot, Super Cayenne, Mitla, Big Chile, Tam Mild Jalepeno, Thai Hot Dragon, Fajita Bell, Mucho Nacho

Potatoes

To Nourish	Anti-inflammation, heart health
In the Kitchen	Mash, bake, roast, add to stews or soups, casseroles.
To Plant	Plant seed potatoes, 12 to 18 inches apart, in furrows, cut side down, 5 inches deep.
To Harvest	Harvest new potatoes when flowers begin to fade. Dig main crop after leaves die back.
Companions	Carrots, leeks, parsley, rosemary
Varieties to Grow	Carola, Gold Rush, Kennebec, Red Norland, Red Pontiac, Superior, Yukon Gold

Pumpkin

To Nourish	Anti-inflammation
In the Kitchen	Bake into dessert, roast seeds.
To Plant	Start seeds indoors. Transplant seedlings, 24 to 60 inches apart, directly into garden.
To Harvest	Harvest pumpkins before frost. Ready to pick when skin is fully colored and hard, vine stem is shriveling. Cut pumpkin with sharp knife, leaving an inch of stem at minimum.
Companions	Winter squash, sweet potato, onions, peppers
Varieties to Grow	**Mini:** Wee-b-Little, Munchkin, Baby Bear **Pie:** Triple Treat, Oz, Trickster **Field/Carving:** Rocket, Howden, Lumina, Connecticut Field, Big Max, Face, Harvest Moon, Ghost Rider, Long Face

Radish

To Nourish	Anti-inflammation
In the Kitchen	Slice and add to salads, eat raw with hummus, roast.
To Plant	Cool season vegetable. Plant seeds, 1 to 6 inches apart, directly into garden.
To Harvest	Harvest when radish is 1 inch diameter.
Companions	Leaf lettuce, carrots, chives, mint
Varieties to Grow	**Spring:** Scarlet Knight, Cheriette, Cherry Belle, Red King, Champion, Pink Beauty, White Icicle **Fall:** All Seasons White, Summer Cross, April Cross, Red Meat, Misato Green

Rhubarb

To Nourish	Anti-inflammation
In the Kitchen	Use in desserts.
To Plant	Plant root stalks, 36 to 60 inches apart, directly into garden.
To Harvest	Harvest stems starting the second growing season. Choose stems that are 12 to 18 inches long and bright red, then cut near base.
Companions	Strawberries, beets, parsley
Varieties to Grow	Chipman's Canada Red, Valentine

Rutabaga

To Nourish	Anti-inflammation
In the Kitchen	Add in soups, stews or casseroles. Roast.
To Plant	Cool season vegetable. Plant seeds, 12 to 18 inches apart, directly into garden.
To Harvest	Leaves are edible, but pick only a few at a time. Pull roots as needed once 3 to 5 inches in diameter.
Companions	Carrots, potatoes, parsnips, parsley
Varieties to Grow	American Purple Top, Laurentian

Scallions

To Nourish	Anti-inflammation
In the Kitchen	Slice thinly and use in pasta, stir-fry, salads.
To Plant	Cool season vegetable. Plant seeds 1 inch apart directly into garden.
To Harvest	Harvest any time after leaves turn green but before bulbs grow wider than the leaves.
Companions	Potatoes, leaf lettuce, strawberries, green peas
Varieties to Grow	Tokyo Long White, White Lisbon

Spinach

To Nourish	Anti-inflammation, healthy digestion, heart health
In the Kitchen	Toss into a salad, use in casseroles, dips, smoothies, vegetable sautés.
To Plant	Cool season vegetable. Plant seeds, 12 inches apart, directly into garden.
To Harvest	Pick leaves as soon as they are big enough to eat, choosing outer ones first. Pull entire plant to harvest leaves just before it bolts (seeds out) in hotter weather.
Companions	Strawberries, scallions, leaf lettuce, green peas
Varieties to Grow	Indian Summer, Malabar, Tyee, Bloomsdale, Longstanding, Correnta

Swiss Chard

To Nourish	Anti-inflammation
In the Kitchen	Add to pasta, eggs, soup, stir-fry, pizza, or stews.
To Plant	Cool season vegetable. Plant seeds, 12 to 18 inches apart, directly into garden.
To Harvest	Pick leaves as soon as they are big enough to harvest, choosing outer leaves first.
Companions	Onions, kale, broccoli, peppers
Varieties to Grow	Bright Lights, Lucullus, Perpetual, Rhubarb

Summer Squash and Zucchini

To Nourish	Anti-inflammation
In the Kitchen	Pasta, soups, stews, add to salads.
To Plant	Start seeds indoors. Transplant seedlings, 36 to 48 inches apart, directly into garden.
To Harvest	Blossoms are edible. Harvest squash at any size, the younger, the more tender the taste, leaving an inch or two of the stem attached when cutting.
Companions	Tomatoes, onions, peppers, eggplant
Varieties to Grow	Eight Ball, Zucchini Select, Elite, Spacemiser, Gold Rush, Burpee Hybrid, Sunburst, Zephyr

Winter Squash

To Nourish	Anti-inflammation, healthy digestion, heart health
In the Kitchen	Stews and soups, mash and serve, cube and roast.
To Plant	Start seeds indoors. Transplant seedlings, 36 to 72 inches apart, directly into garden.
To Harvest	Blossoms are edible. Pick squash when rind is fully colored and hard, but before frost.
Companions	Kale, turnip, sage, thyme
Varieties to Grow	**Bush style:** Cream of the Crop **Vining:** Early Butternut, Table Ace, Festival, Sweet Mama, Ponca, Carnival, Table Queen, Buttercup, Baby Blue Hubbard, Ambercup, Blue Ballet, Sweet Meat

Sweet Potato

To Nourish	Healthy digestion, anti-inflammation, heart health
In the Kitchen	Roast, boil and mash. Cut slices and grill. Cube and roast.
To Plant	Plant seed potatoes, 12 to 18 inches apart, directly into garden furrows.
To Harvest	Harvest when ends of vines turn yellow, before first frost. Tubers are shallow so dig with hands carefully.
Companions	Carrots, spinach, green beans, cilantro
Varieties to Grow	Centennial, Georgia Jet, Porto Rico, Vardaman

Strawberries

To Nourish	Anti-inflammation, heart health
In the Kitchen	Add to salads, fruit parfaits, desserts, breakfast, and smoothies.
To Plant	Plant roots, 6 to 18 inches apart, directly into garden.
To Harvest	Pick in morning when fruits are cool.
Companions	Leaf lettuce, spinach, scallions, rhubarb
Varieties to Grow	June Bearing: Annapolis, Itasca, Jewel, Mesabi, Sable, Winona

Tomato

To Nourish	Anti-inflammation, heart health
In the Kitchen	Pasta, soup, stews, salads, salsa, and sauces.
To Plant	Start seeds indoors. Transplant seedlings, 24 to 36 inches apart, directly into garden, burying ⅔ of the plant during planting. Add a cage to support the plant.
To Harvest	Pick when tomatoes show deep color, and are firm.
Companions	Basil, parsley, eggplant, garlic, marigolds
Varieties to Grow	**Small fruit size:** Tumbler, Sweet 100, Patio Hybrid, Early Cascade, Oregon Spring, Juliet, Vita Gold, Sweet Million, Sweet Chelsea, Container Choice, Viva Italia, Square Paste **Regular fruit size:** Quick Pick, Bush Celebrity, Johnny's 361, Redrider, OG50 Whopper, Roadside Red, Sunrise, Golden Girl, Mountain Pride, Celebrity, Lemon Boy, Supersteak, Brandywine, Golden Jubilee, Royal Mountie, Sunshine, Sunstart

Turnips

To Nourish	Anti-inflammation
In the Kitchen	Use the same way as potatoes or kohlrabi. Bake, boil, stews, soups, Add to salads, eat raw.
To Plant	Plant seeds, 4 inches apart, directly into garden.
To Harvest	Clip turnip greens when young (less than 12 inches long). Pull roots when turnip is 1 to 2 inches in diameter.
Companions	Onions, potatoes, thyme, carrots
Varieties to Grow	Tokyo Cross Hybrid, Purple Top White Globe

Watermelon

To Nourish	Anti-inflammation, heart health
In the Kitchen	Slice and eat raw, make a salad, or fruity punch.
To Plant	Start seeds indoors or directly plant seeds into garden in a hill, 36 to 60 inches apart.
To Harvest	Pick melons when belly touching the soil is yellow and rind becomes dull in color. Rapping on rind should produce a low-pitched thud. Ripe melons slip easily from the vine.
Companions	Corn, onions, mint, cantaloupe
Varieties to Grow	Festival, Sugar Baby, New Queen Jubilation

Create the recipe to a nourishing life:

Which fruits and vegetables will you plant to help you and your family to a more nourishing life?

Which fruits or vegetables have you never tried before?

Which fruits or vegetables are essential to your garden of nourishment?

Think about the recipes you wish to make when you bring in the harvest together. Jot them down here.

CHAPTER 8

PLANTING FOR YOUR PLATE

Every time we eat is an opportunity to nourish ourselves.

~Unknown

One year we decided to divide our garden into four areas featuring foods from different recipes we enjoyed as a family. There was the "Taco Tuesday" section which featured tomatoes, peppers, and onions. There was the "Stir-fry" section, which grew cabbages, carrots, and peas. My kids came up with the "All-American" section for our weekly pizza nights featuring tomatoes, basil, and eggplant. And the fourth area, "Pasta and Salad Garden," included kitchen staples like broccoli, zucchini, lettuce, spinach, and cucumbers.

Creating these themes gave us a logical planning guide for our summer meal schedule. Just like when I was a child, the question of *"What's for dinner?"* meant running to the garden to see what was ready to harvest. This created a true sense of "garden-to-plate" eating, where my kids harvested the fruits and vegetables they planted weeks before, and we combined those foods into a recipe which brought us all around the table together. We were planting for our plates.

When you incorporate your family's favorite recipes into garden planning and planting, enhancing the nutrition of your family follows naturally. When you create gardens that nourish your kitchens with the food your family loves, it's almost certain that food will nourish your family as well. Gathering your family together to plan what fruits and vegetables belong in your favorite recipes also entices kids to want to eat those fruits and vegetables.

Do you have a weekly menu theme for your family? Choose what your family loves and brainstorm which foods you can grow to be a part of the recipe. Planting for your plates guides your menu planning, and can simplify a busy summer schedule. It's a tool to help you become more organized and intentional about the foods you want to plant and nourish your family with. Gather your family and create a garden filled with food your family will enjoy all summer long.

Do you need some inspiration? Here are some ideas:

Wake-Up for Breakfast Garden

Maybe your family loves breakfast. Whether you prefer smoothies, fresh melon cups, egg dishes, or breakfast tacos, waking up to these fruits and vegetables will provide the ingredients to a nourishing morning meal. You might even find something here to make breakfast for dinner!

- Berries (strawberries, raspberries, blackberries)
- Kale
- Spinach
- Melon (cantaloupe, watermelon, honeydew)
- Carrots
- Sweet potatoes
- Onions
- Peppers
- Potatoes

Salad Garden

Imagine going through the summer without having to buy lettuce at the supermarket. You can if you plant these ingredients! Keep planting the greens every two to three weeks for continuous harvesting. A salad garden can also encourage your kids to build a leafy creation every night for the evening meal.

- Lettuce
- Swiss Chard
- Kale
- Spinach
- Arugula
- Cucumbers
- Tomatoes
- Beets
- Carrots
- Radishes

Salsa Garden

Salsa can be an ingredient in breakfast, lunch, or dinner recipes. With so many variations—corn salsa, pineapple salsa, and of course, garden fresh salsa—you will never run out of combinations. You can even plant enough to preserve through canning or invite the neighbors over! Summer salsa is coming right up!

- Tomatoes
- Cilantro
- Bell Peppers
- Hot Peppers
- Yellow or White Onions
- Garlic
- Corn

Kitchen Garden

Kitchen gardens have a little bit of everything in them, based on what you use frequently in your kitchen. Plant what you tend to buy a lot of at the supermarket.

- Onions
- Carrots
- Cucumbers
- Cabbage
- Broccoli and cauliflower
- Potatoes and sweet potatoes
- Bell Peppers
- Spinach
- Lettuce
- Tomatoes
- Zucchini and summer squash
- Kale
- Celery
- Green Beans
- Peas and snow peas
- Corn

Pizza Garden

Is Sunday night pizza night at your house? These ingredients will make a flavorful pizza in the oven or on the grill. Whether it's southwestern-style pizza, barbecue chicken pizza, or traditional pizza, you won't want to skip out on these ingredients. Consider planting fresh herbs too!

- Tomatoes
- Sweet Bell Peppers
- Zucchini
- Eggplant
- Beets
- Onions
- Cilantro
- Oregano
- Basil

Pasta and Salad Garden

Whether your family likes chicken Alfredo, spaghetti, eggplant parmesan, or pasta primavera, here are some favorite vegetables from those recipes. You could even try a weekly pasta bar with all of these ingredients. Cook up the pasta and set out the toppings...and don't forget the salad!

- Tomatoes
- Bell peppers
- Lettuce
- Cucumbers
- Broccoli
- Zucchini
- Peas
- Carrots
- Eggplant
- Onions
- Spinach
- Basil

Taco Garden

Does your family like Mexican favorites like tacos and burritos? Try incorporating garden-fresh ingredients into your favorite recipes, experimenting with some new ways to celebrate the well-loved taco, like burrito bowls, fish tacos, taco salad, or even nachos. The ideas are endless.

- Tomatoes
- Lettuce
- Corn
- Cilantro
- Bell Peppers
- Hot Peppers
- Onions

Stir-Fry Garden

With temperatures rising outside in the summer, this meal won't heat up the kitchen inside. Stir-fry meals are quick, simple, and filled with vegetables. Keep it simple and just make one batch for the whole family or schedule a stir-fry night where everyone selects their own vegetables and builds their own stir-fry. It's all about customization!

- Cabbage
- Onions
- Carrots
- Peas (all types)
- Bell peppers
- Hot peppers
- Broccoli
- Cauliflower
- Summer squash
- Zucchini

Container Garden

While not a theme itself, you may want to try planting a few vegetables in containers so they can be ready when you are cooking in the kitchen. Almost any vegetable that will grow in a typical backyard garden will also grow well in a container. Here's a list of container-loving vegetables:

- Broccoli
- Carrots
- Cucumbers
- Eggplant
- Green Beans
- Green Onions
- Leaf Lettuce
- Peppers
- Radish
- Spinach
- Squash
- Tomato
- Turnip

Herb Garden

Herb gardens not only add zest to our vegetable gardens with their fragrance, but they can also add flavor and antioxidants to our plates. Maybe you enjoy making basil pesto for pasta or having the neighbors over for nacho night with fresh salsa and guacamole topped with cilantro. Either way, grow the herbs that go with your family's favorite foods. To begin with, choose herbs you often buy fresh at the supermarket. Growing herbs in the garden can be a fun way to motivate the family to cook together as well, since touching and gently rubbing the leaves of the herb plant will release the aroma. That scent will surely develop into a recipe. Here are some favorites:

- Parsley
- Basil
- Cilantro
- Thyme
- Rosemary
- Marjoram
- Mint
- Oregano
- Chives
- Tarragon

Planning a Garden for Your Plate:

Over a family meal, discuss your family's favorite meals.

Brainstorm which ingredients could be grown in the family garden that are found in their favorite meals.

Which gardens will you plant for your plate?

CHAPTER 9

RECIPES FOR YOUR TABLE

You don't have to cook fancy complicated masterpieces, just good food from fresh ingredients. ~Julia Child

Harvesting your own fresh vegetables and fruits from the garden is exciting. You've grown them as a family and now you get to enjoy them as a family. The ultimate reward is gathering around the table to eat the foods your hands worked to grow. I hope you savor these recipes with your family both in the kitchen as you prepare them together and around the table as you eat them together.

Breakfast Recipes

Wake-Up Smoothie

Serves 4

Ingredients

- 2 to 3 cups fresh or frozen berries (any)
- 2 ripe bananas
- 1 handful fresh spinach, about 1 cup
- 1 cup Greek vanilla or strawberry yogurt
- 1 cup strawberry and banana puree
- ½ cup milk
- 2 tablespoons chia seed, if desired

Directions

1. Add all ingredients to blender and process until smooth.

Note: Using frozen berries will create a colder, icier beverage. Substitute frozen peaches in place of berries, if desired, or use a mixture of the two. Strawberry banana puree is found in the refrigerator section of the grocery store, sold under brands like Naked Juice® or Bolthouse Farms®.

Muffin Egg Frittatas

Makes 24 mini muffins

Ingredients

- 6 eggs
- ½ cup fat-free milk
- ¼ teaspoon salt
- ⅛ teaspoon black pepper
- 1 cup shredded reduced-fat cheddar cheese
- 1 tablespoon canola oil
- 1 ¼ cup chopped vegetables such as onions, zucchini, peppers

Directions

1. Heat oven to 350°F. Beat eggs, milk, salt, and black pepper in medium bowl until blended. Stir in shredded cheese. Set aside.

2. Heat pan over medium-high heat on stovetop; add canola oil and vegetables. Sauté for 3 to 5 minutes. Add vegetables to egg mixture.

3. Spoon egg mixture into greased mini muffin tins. Bake 10 to 12 minutes or until light golden brown. Cool 2 to 3 minutes and serve.

Chicken Sausage Scramble

Makes 4 servings

Ingredients

- Non-stick cooking spray
- ½ cup diced chicken and apple sausage links
- ¼ cup diced onion
- ¼ cup diced red pepper
- ¼ cup diced sweet potato
- 4 eggs
- 2 tablespoons fat-free milk
- ½ cup chopped fresh spinach leaves
- Salt and black pepper, to taste
- 2 whole wheat English muffins, split and toasted

Directions

1. Coat a nonstick skillet with nonstick spray; heat over medium. Add the sausage, onion, red pepper, and sweet potato and cook, covered, stirring often, until vegetables are tender (test a chunk of sweet potato to be sure).

2. Meanwhile, beat eggs with milk in a small bowl until blended. When the vegetables are tender, transfer them to a plate. Return the skillet to the burner. Add the egg mixture and cook, stirring often, until eggs are softly scrambled.

Off heat, stir in spinach, reserved sausage mixture, salt, and pepper. Serve immediately with a toasted English muffin half.

Notes: Chicken apple sausage links are lower fat options that can be found in the health food section of the supermarket. This recipe was a favorite in my cooking classes and is courtesy of Midwest Dairy. Turn this into a breakfast sandwich by simply placing the scramble on the toasted English muffin.

Breakfast Casserole

Serves 12-16

Ingredients

- 2 tablespoons olive oil
- 3 cups cut-up vegetables, peppers, onions, shredded carrots, broccoli florets
- 8 large eggs
- 2 cups fat-free milk
- 2 cups shredded, reduced-fat cheddar cheese, divided
- 2 cups frozen hash brown potatoes, thawed in refrigerator
- 1 cup diced ham

Directions

1. Preheat oven to 350°F. Spray 9 x 13 inch dish or two 9-inch pie plates with non-stick cooking spray.
2. Add oil to large non-stick skillet over medium heat, add vegetables and stir occasionally until tender, about 8 minutes.
3. Whisk eggs with milk in large bowl. Stir in 1 ½ cups cheese, cooked vegetables, potatoes, and ham. Pour into prepared baking dish(es).
4. Cover with aluminum foil and bake 40 minutes. Uncover and sprinkle with remaining

cheese and bake another 20 to 30 minutes or
until eggs are thoroughly cooked.

Notes: Any combination of garden vegetables will
work well here. Feel free to add fresh herbs if desired.

Salads

Build Your Own Salad Bar

Adding a salad to every evening meal is a great way to encourage your family to eat more fruits and vegetables. Set out ingredients to for everyone to make their own salad creation, or let them choose individual items with salad dressing as a dip.

Start with Leafy Greens:
- Arugula, green or red leaf lettuce, mixed greens, cabbage, romaine, spinach, kale.

Add vegetables:
- Beets, bell peppers, broccoli, cauliflower, carrots, celery, corn, cucumbers, onions, peas, radishes, peas, tomatoes, zucchini slices.

Add fruits:
- Dried cranberries, apples, blueberries, grapes, mandarin oranges, cantaloupe, honeydew pears, raisins, strawberries.

Add beans:
- Black beans, edamame, kidney beans, navy beans, chickpeas.

Sprinkle on extras:

- Cheese, almonds, cashews, peanuts, pecans, walnuts, avocado, bacon bits, sunflower seeds.

Add chopped fresh herbs for flavor, if desired:

- Cilantro, basil, thyme, chives, oregano

To create a main dish salad, add:

- Cooked ground beef with taco seasonings
- Grilled chicken
- Hard-cooked eggs
- Grilled or broiled salmon
- Grilled shrimp
- Tuna or chicken salad
- Cubed ham or diced turkey

Try these combinations:

- Romaine, tomatoes, cucumbers, carrots, avocado, and shrimp
- Mixed greens, grilled chicken, honeydew or cantaloupe, walnuts, and feta cheese
- Spinach, apples, walnuts, white cheddar cheese, grilled chicken, and dried cranberries
- Romaine, seasoned ground beef, tomatoes, corn, black beans, cheddar cheese, and salsa

Fresh Broccoli and Bacon Salad

Serves 6

Ingredients

- ¼ cup low-fat mayonnaise
- ¼ cup non-fat plain Greek yogurt
- 2 teaspoons cider vinegar
- 1 teaspoon sugar
- 4 cups finely chopped broccoli
- 3 slices cooked bacon, crumbled
- 3 tablespoons dried cranberries
- Freshly ground pepper to taste

Directions

1. Whisk mayonnaise, Greek yogurt, vinegar, and sugar in a large bowl. Add broccoli, bacon, dried cranberries, and pepper; stir to coat with the dressing.

Notes: To make ahead, cover and refrigerate for up to one day.

Salmon Berry Salad with Citrus Vinaigrette

Serves 2

Ingredients

Vinaigrette:

- ⅓ cup olive oil
- ⅓ cup orange juice
- 1 tablespoon sugar
- 1 teaspoon ground cinnamon
- 1 teaspoon ground ginger
- ⅛ teaspoon salt

Salad:

- 2 – 5 ounce salmon fillets
- 4 cups fresh baby spinach leaves
- 1 cup blueberries
- 1 cup sliced strawberries
- ¼ cup toasted pecan pieces

Directions

1. For the vinaigrette, mix all ingredients in small bowl until well-blended.

2. Refrigerate ½ of the vinaigrette to use as a dressing. Place salmon in large re-sealable plastic bag or dish. Add remaining vinaigrette and toss to coat well.

3. Refrigerate 30 minutes. Remove salmon from marinade and discard marinade.

4. Grill or broil over medium-high heating 5 minutes per side or until salmon flakes easily in the center.

5. Divide spinach, berries, and pecans among two plates. Arrange salmon fillet over salad. Whisk reserved vinaigrette. Drizzle over salads.

Spinach Fruit Salad with Strawberry Poppy Seed Dressing

Serves 6

Ingredients

- 4 cups spinach leaves
- 2 cups fresh sliced strawberries, divided
- 1 cup diced cantaloupe
- ¼ cup walnut pieces
- 1 tablespoon sugar
- 1 tablespoon raspberry vinegar
- ⅓ cup lemon yogurt
- ¾ tsp poppy or chia seeds

Directions

- In a medium serving bowl, combine spinach, 1 ½ cups strawberries and cantaloupe. Top with walnut pieces.
1. In blender, combine ½ cup strawberries, sugar, vinegar, yogurt, and poppy seeds. Blend until smooth.
2. Pour dressing over salad and toss gently coating salad ingredients.

Fruity Chardy Salad

Serves 4

Ingredients

- 4 to 6 Swiss chard leaves
- 2 cups spinach
- 2 cups sliced strawberries
- 2 cups diced cantaloupe
- 4 to 6 tablespoons raspberry vinaigrette

Directions

2. Thoroughly wash Swiss chard leaves and spinach. To prepare Swiss chard, remove center rib of leaf and tear remaining leaves into bite-size pieces. Place in medium bowl.

3. Top leafy greens with strawberries and cantaloupe. Drizzle with vinaigrette. Toss and serve.

Salsas and Dips

Fresh Garden Salsa

Serves 6

Ingredients

- 3 cups diced fresh tomatoes
- ½ cup diced green pepper
- 1 jalapeño pepper, finely diced
- 1 cup fresh cilantro
- ½ red onion, diced
- 1 tablespoon vinegar
- ¼ cup olive oil
- Juice of 2 limes

Directions

1. Combine all ingredients in bowl, stir to blend well. Refrigerate until chilled or serve immediately.

Pineapple Salsa

Serves 7

Ingredients

- 2 cups chopped fresh pineapple
- 1 cup chopped red pepper
- ½ cup diced yellow onion
- ¼ cup lemon or lime juice
- 3 tablespoons chopped cilantro
- 1 to 2 fresh jalapeno peppers, seeded and finely chopped

Directions

1. Combine pineapple, bell pepper, onion, lemon or lime juice, cilantro and jalapeno pepper in medium bowl.

2. For a richer flavor, cover and refrigerate for 4 to 24 hours, stirring occasionally. Serve with grilled chicken or seafood or as an appetizer with chips.

Roasted Corn Salsa

Serves 7

Ingredients

- 2 large ears yellow sweet corn-on-the-cob (to yield 1 ¼ cups cut corn)
- 1 tablespoon olive oil
- ½ cup finely chopped red onion
- ½ cup finely chopped ripe tomato
- 1 jalapeno pepper, seeds removed and finely chopped
- ¼ cup diced green bell pepper
- ¼ cup finely chopped cilantro
- 1 to 2 tablespoons fresh lime juice
- ½ to 1 teaspoon ground cumin
- ⅛ teaspoon salt and black pepper, to taste

Directions

1. Cut kernels from ear to measure 1 ¼ cups. Toss the corn into a preheated sauté pan with 1 tablespoon olive oil to roast for 3 to 4 minutes. Let cool.

2. Combine corn with chopped onion, tomato, jalapeño pepper, bell pepper, and cilantro. Add lime juice and cumin to taste; then stir in salt and ground pepper. Cover and chill, allowing flavors to blend for about 15 minutes or more.

Peachy Chipotle Salsa

Serves 6

Ingredients

- 2 cups diced ripe peaches
- ¾ cup fresh lemon juice
- ½ cup diced red onion
- ½ cup diced red bell pepper
- ¼ cup canned chipotle chili peppers, seeded and minced
- 1 ½ teaspoons minced garlic
- ½ teaspoon ground cumin
- ½ teaspoon minced fresh oregano or ¼ teaspoon dried ground oregano
- ⅛ teaspoon salt
- ⅛ teaspoon freshly ground black pepper

Directions

1. Combine all ingredients in a large bowl. Cover and refrigerate for up to 3 days. Delicious over baked fish, chicken, or pork.

Greek Six-Layer Dip

Serves 15

Ingredients

- 1 – 6 ounce container plain Greek yogurt
- 1 clove garlic, minced
- 1 ½ teaspoons dried dill weed
- 2 teaspoons lemon juice
- ¼ teaspoon kosher salt
- 2 cups roasted red pepper hummus
- ¾ cup chopped cucumber
- 1 cup quartered cherry or grape tomatoes
- ½ cup sliced olives
- ½ cup crumbled feta cheese

Directions

1. In a small bowl, combine yogurt, garlic, dill, lemon juice, and salt. Set aside. Spread hummus onto 12-inch platter. Layer yogurt mixture over hummus.
2. Top with cucumbers, tomatoes, olives and feta cheese. Serve with whole grain chips.

Note: This recipe was adapted from a favorite Hy-Vee recipe that was popular at cooking classes.

Creamy Guacamole

Makes 3 cups

Ingredients

- 4 avocados, halved, seeded and divided
- ½ cup nonfat plain Greek yogurt
- 2 tablespoons chopped red onion
- 2 tablespoons chopped cilantro leaves
- 2 teaspoons fresh lime juice
- ½ fresh jalapeño pepper, seeded and chopped
- 1 clove garlic, chopped
- ½ teaspoon salt

Directions

1. Place pulp of 2 avocados, yogurt, onion, cilantro, lime juice, jalapeño, garlic, salt, and lime juice in a medium food processor. Pulse process the mixture until well blended and creamy.

2. Cut remaining 2 avocados into medium-size chunks. Add avocados to processor. Pulse process just until blended leaving some chunks of avocado. Cover with plastic wrap directly on top of the guacamole. Chill 1 hour to allow flavors to blend.

Note: This recipe comes from my friends at Midwest Dairy and was featured on one of my television segments.

Southwestern Layered Bean Dip

Serves 12-15

Ingredients

- 1 – 16 ounce can nonfat refried beans
- 1 – 15 ounce can black beans, drained and rinsed
- 4 green onions, sliced
- ½ cup salsa
- ½ teaspoon ground cumin
- ½ teaspoon chili powder
- ¼ cup finely diced jalapeño peppers
- 1 cup shredded reduced-fat pepperjack cheese
- ½ cup non-fat plain Greek yogurt
- 1 ½ cups shredded romaine or iceburg lettuce
- 1 medium tomato, chopped
- 1 medium avocado, diced

Directions

1. Combine refried beans, black beans, onions, salsa, cumin, chili powder, and jalapeños in a medium bowl. Transfer to a shallow 2-quart microwave-safe dish; sprinkle with cheese.

2. Microwave on high 3 minutes or until cheese melts and beans are hot. Spread yogurt evenly over the hot bean mixture, then sprinkle with shredded lettuce, tomato, and avocado.

Vegetables and Main Dishes

Honey-Roasted Root Vegetables

Serves 8

Ingredients

- 2 cups coarsely chopped, peeled sweet potatoes
- 1 ½ cups coarsely chopped, peeled turnip
- 1 ½ cups coarsely chopped, peeled parsnip
- 1 ½ cups coarsely chopped carrot
- ¼ cup honey
- 2 tablespoons olive oil
- ½ teaspoon salt
- 3 onions, halved

Directions

1. Preheat oven to 450°F.
2. Combine all ingredients in large bowl; toss to coat all of the vegetables.
3. Place mixture on a large pan coated with cooking spray.
4. Bake 35 minutes or until vegetables are tender and begin to brown, stirring every 15 minutes.

Spring Vegetable Sauté

Serves 6

Ingredients

- 2 tablespoons olive oil
- ¼ cup diced onion
- 1 garlic clove, minced
- 3 cups sliced vegetables, such as zucchini, green beans, asparagus, red bell peppers, carrots, celery
- 2 tablespoons fresh chopped basil
- Salt and black pepper to taste

Directions

1. Heat oil in large skillet over medium heat and sauté onion and garlic for one minute. Add vegetables while reducing heat to low, stirring constantly until tender yet firm, about five minutes.

2. Sprinkle with basil and season with salt and pepper. Remove from heat. Serve warm.

Spicy Grilled Sweet Potatoes

Serves 4

Ingredients

- ¾ tsp ground cumin
- ½ teaspoon garlic powder
- ¼ teaspoon salt
- ⅛ teaspoon black pepper
- 1 tablespoon olive oil
- 1 pound peeled sweet potatoes, cut into ¼ inch slices
- 2 tablespoons fresh chopped cilantro

Directions

1. In a small bowl, stir cumin, garlic powder, salt, and black pepper.
2. Heat a large grill pan coated with nonstick cooking spray over medium heat.
3. Add potatoes; cook 10 minutes, turning occasionally.
4. Place potatoes in a large bowl, sprinkle with cumin mixture and cilantro. Toss gently coating potatoes.

BBQ Chicken and Cheesy Potatoes Foil Dinner

Serves 4

Ingredients

- 4 tablespoons barbeque sauce, divided
- 4 small boneless, skinless chicken breast halves
- 4 red potatoes, thinly sliced, divided
- 1 red or green bell pepper, seeded and sliced, divided
- 1 cup chopped yellow onion
- Salt and black pepper, to taste
- 1 ½ cups shredded reduced-fat cheddar cheese, divided

Directions

1. Preheat grill to medium heat.
2. Place a foil sheet, approximately 12 x 12-inches, on a work surface. Spray with non-stick cooking spray.
3. Spoon about 1 ½ tablespoon barbecue sauce in the center of the foil sheet. Place one chicken breast half over barbecue sauce, and spread another 1 ½ tablespoon of sauce over chicken. Top with a fourth of the sliced potato, bell

peppers, and onion. Season with salt and pepper.

4. Fold foil in half to cover contents; make narrow folds along edges to seal.

5. Repeat with remaining ingredients to assemble three more packets. Place packets on grill.

6. Open foil packets with scissors and carefully pull back edges (contents may be very hot).

7. Sprinkle a quarter of the cheese over the top of each chicken breast half and return to grill or campfire, unsealed, for 2 minutes or until cheese is melted.

Notes: You can also cook these packets over a campfire for approximately 30 minutes. If you desire to cook inside in the oven, set heat to 375°F and bake for 30 minutes or until temperature of chicken reaches 165°F. This recipe was adapted from Midwest Dairy.

MyPlate Pizza

Serves 4

Ingredients

- Pizza dough, divided
- ½ cup pizza sauce or pesto sauce
- 1 cup shredded mozzarella cheese
- 1 cup chopped vegetables (broccoli florets, cauliflower florets, shredded carrots, zucchini slices, bell pepper slices, quartered or sliced tomatoes)
- ½ cup Parmesan cheese

Directions

1. Heat oven to 425°F. Divide pizza dough evenly into four sections. Roll out each piece into a small circle, approximately 4 to 5 inches around.

2. Spread each dough piece with sauce, mozzarella cheese, an assortment of vegetables and Parmesan cheese. Place on pizza stone or large pan.

3. Bake for 10 minutes or until cheese begins to turn golden. Serve.

Cauliflower Macaroni and Cheese

Serves 6

Ingredients

- 1 ½ cups dry whole grain elbow macaroni
- 1 cup fresh cauliflower florets
- Small amount of water
- Non-stick cooking spray
- 1 tablespoon olive oil
- 1 tablespoon all-purpose flour
- ½ cup milk
- 1 ½ cups shredded cheddar cheese
- 4 ounces lite cream cheese, softened
- ½ teaspoon salt
- ⅛ teaspoon black pepper
- ⅛ teaspoon paprika

Directions

1. Bring a large pot of water to boil and cook macaroni according to package directions. Drain in colander, set aside.

2. Meanwhile, steam broccoli in a pan with a small amount of water for 4-6 minutes over medium heat. Once cooked, add cauliflower and small amount of water to a blender. Puree until mixture reaches a smooth and creamy texture, adding additional water as needed.

3. Coat a large saucepan with cooking spray and heat over medium. Add oil, then flour and cook, stirring constantly, for one minute until mixture resembles a thick paste but has not browned.

4. To saucepan, add milk and whisk until mixture begins to thicken, approximately three minutes. Add vegetable puree, cheese, cream cheese and seasonings and stir until cheese is melted. Add cooked pasta and stir well. Serve.

Ultimate Teriyaki Beef and Vegetable Rice Bowls

Serves 4 to 6

Ingredients

- 2 tablespoons Wok oil, divided
- 1 head Napa cabbage, shredded
- 1 green bell pepper, sliced or diced
- 1 onion, sliced
- 1 head broccoli, cut into bite-size florets
- 1 pound sirloin steak, cut into very thin strips
- 1 cup teriyaki sauce, such as Soy Vay Island Teriyaki
- 4 to 6 cups cooked Jasmine rice
- 3 green onions, thinly sliced on the diagonal

Directions

1. Over medium high heat, add one tablespoon of wok oil to large non-stick pan and toss in cabbage, bell pepper, onion, and broccoli. Sauté 5 minutes or until vegetables begin to caramelize while remaining crisp. Remove from pan and keep warm.

2. Over medium-high heat, add remaining tablespoon wok oil and sauté half of the beef to avoid overcrowding. Cook quickly stirring

frequently, approximately 2 minutes. Remove cooked beef and repeat with remaining beef. Remove from pan.

3. Decrease heat to medium and add teriyaki sauce to pan. Add all beef back to pan to evenly coat. Pour beef and sauce over hot rice and top with hot cooked vegetables. Garnish with chopped green onions.

Notes: The best cuts of beef for stir-frying are top sirloin, sirloin tip steak, flat iron steak and flank steak. For easier slicing of beef, place beef in freezer for 30 minutes prior to cutting.

Ultimate Chicken Nachos

Serves 6

Ingredients

- 1 bag whole grain tortilla chips
- 1 tablespoon olive oil
- 1 red bell pepper, chopped
- 1 onion thinly sliced
- 2 cups diced pre-cooked chicken breast or rotisserie chicken
- 1 cup black bean and corn salsa
- 1 cup shredded pepperjack cheese
- Topping: plain, Greek yogurt, cilantro, and chopped green onions

Directions

1. Preheat oven to 350°F. Spread a single layer of tortilla chips on baking pan.
2. Heat oil in a nonstick skillet over medium-high heat. Sauté red bell pepper, stirring constantly, until crisp-tender, about 2 to 3 minutes. Spoon evenly over chips.
3. Combine chicken and salsa in a bowl. Spoon over bell peppers. Sprinkle cheese on top.
4. Bake 5 minutes at 350°F, or until cheese melts.
5. Top with plain, non-fat Greek yogurt, cilantro, and chopped green onions, if desired.

Garden Patch Muffin Tin Pizzas

Serves 12

Ingredients

- 1 – 16 ounce loaf frozen 100% whole wheat bread dough, thawed
- ½ cup finely chopped fresh cherry tomatoes
- ¼ cup finely chopped green pepper
- 2 tablespoons finely chopped broccoli
- 2 tablespoons finely chopped cauliflower
- 4 tablespoons pizza or pesto sauce, divided
- ¾ cup mozzarella cheese, divided

Directions

1. Heat oven to 425°F. Spray a large knife with cooking spray and cut thawed loaf into 12 equal pieces. Flatten each piece into a disk and place in muffin cups sprayed with cooking spray.

2. Combine cherry tomatoes, green pepper, broccoli, and cauliflower in a small bowl.

3. Place 1 teaspoon pizza sauce on crust in each muffin cup. Divide vegetable mixture among pizzas (about 1 heaping tablespoon each) and sprinkle each with 1 tablespoon cheese.

4. Bake for 15 to 17 minutes or until cheese is bubbly and crust is golden brown.

Mexican Pizza Squares

Serves 24

Ingredients

- 2 – 8 ounce packages refrigerated reduced-fat crescent rolls
- 1 – 16 ounce can non-fat refried beans
- 1 cup plain non-fat Greek yogurt
- 2 tablespoons taco seasoning
- ⅓ cup chopped green onion
- 1 green bell pepper, seeded and chopped
- 2 medium tomatoes, chopped
- 1 ½ cups shredded cheddar cheese

Directions

1. Preheat oven to 375°F. Separate crescent roll dough and place on a 15 x 10-inch jelly roll pan. Press perforations together to form crust on bottom and up sides. Bake 15 minutes until golden brown. Let cool.

2. Spread refried beans over crust to within ½ inch of edges.

3. Stir together Greek yogurt and taco seasoning. Spread over bean layer. Top with onions, bell pepper, tomatoes, olives, and cheese. Cover and refrigerate at least 1 hour before serving.

Sweet Thai Chicken Pizza

Serves 4, 2 slices each

Ingredients

- 1 pre-cooked whole-wheat pizza crust
- ¾ cup sweet Thai chili sauce, divided
- 1 cup chopped pre-cooked chicken
- 1 cup thinly sliced red pepper
- ½ cup finely diced fresh pineapple
- 1 ½ cups shredded mozzarella cheese
- ½ cup shredded carrots
- ½ cup shredded zucchini
- 2 tablespoons chopped cilantro
- 2 tablespoons sliced green onions

Directions

1. Preheat oven to 425°F. Brush the pizza crust with ½ cup of the sweet Thai chili sauce.

2. Top evenly with chicken, pepper strips, and pineapple and finish with the mozzarella.

3. Bake 6 to 8 minutes. Let the pizza rest 5 minutes.

4. Sprinkle evenly with the carrots, zucchini, cilantro, and green onions. Drizzle remaining sweet Thai chili sauce over the pizza. Slice and serve.

Grilled Southwest Pizza

Serves 8

Ingredients

- ½ pound boneless skinless chicken breast, pounded thinly
- 2 tablespoons olive oil, divided
- 3 tablespoons taco seasoning, divided
- 1 recipe prepared pizza dough
- Flour, for work surface
- ½ cup mild or medium taco sauce
- 1 to 1 ½ cups shredded reduced-fat Mexican-blend cheese
- 1 cup thinly sliced bell peppers (use a jalapeño if desired)
- Toppings: guacamole, salsa, plain Greek yogurt, cilantro

Directions

1. Place pounded chicken in a bowl with 1 tablespoon olive oil. Toss to coat. Sprinkle 2 tablespoons taco seasoning over chicken and let marinate for 30 minutes in refrigerator. Preheat grill to medium-high heat.
2. Grill 8 to 10 minutes until chicken is cooked through, reaching an internal temperature of 165°F. Remove from grill, cool, and dice.

3. Divide dough into thirds. Roll out on lightly floured surface until ¼-inch thick. Brush each pizza crust lightly with 1 teaspoon olive oil. Sprinkle lightly with remaining taco seasoning, if desired. Add dough to hot grill and cook for 3 minutes. Check dough by using tongs to lift. Flip when bubbles are forming on the top of the dough and grill marks are appearing. Cook an additional 2 to 3 minutes. Remove from grill.

4. Evenly and lightly spread taco sauce, cheese, chicken and peppers over three pizzas. Return pizzas briefly to the grill, cover and cook until cheese is melted.

5. Top with guacamole, salsa, plain Greek yogurt, and cilantro.

Pasta Faggioli

Serves 8

Ingredients

- 1 ½ teaspoons olive oil
- 1 pound ground beef, 90% lean
- 1 onion, diced
- 3 carrots, diced
- 3 stalks celery, diced
- 24 ounces canned diced tomatoes
- 2 cups canned red or white kidney beans, drained and rinsed
- 6 cups beef stock, no added sodium
- 1 ½ teaspoons oregano
- 1 ¼ teaspoons black pepper
- 2 ½ teaspoons fresh chopped parsley
- ¾ teaspoon hot pepper sauce
- 1 – 26 ounce jar spaghetti sauce
- ½ cup dry pasta, such as orzo

Directions

1. Heat oil to medium in non-stick pan. Add beef and cook thoroughly.
2. Add onion, carrots and celery. Sauté for 5 minutes.
3. Stir in tomatoes, beans, beef stock, spices, hot sauce, and spaghetti sauce. Simmer until

carrots and celery are cooked through, approximately 20 minutes.

4. Add pasta the last 8 minutes of cooking. Serve with warm bread.

Taco Rice Bowls

Serves 6.

Ingredients

- 6 flour tortillas
- 1 pound extra lean ground beef
- 2 cups precooked brown rice
- 3 tablespoons taco seasoning
- ¼ cup water
- 2 cups shredded lettuce
- 1 to 2 fresh tomatoes, diced
- 4 ounces shredded cheddar cheese

Directions

1. Preheat oven to 350°F. Using a muffin tin, fold tortillas into a circular shape and place in muffin tin to hold. Repeat with remaining tortillas and bake 5 to 7 minutes or until crisp. Remove from oven and set aside.

2. Meanwhile, brown beef in skillet until thoroughly cooked. Add taco seasoning and ¼ cup water. Stir in cooked rice.

3. Spoon rice mixture into tortilla muffin shells and top with lettuce, tomatoes, and cheese.

Note: This recipe was my daughter's entry into the Uncle Ben's Cooking Contest for Kids. It is a sure family favorite.

CHAPTER 10

CREATE YOUR RECIPE

A recipe is a story that ends with a good meal.

~Pat Conroy Sarton

I remember the struggle of putting my kids to bed when they were babies—rocking and cradling and pleading for them to sleep—when all they wanted was to stay nuzzled in my arms comfy, cozy, and warm. Then, almost overnight, all of that baby holding changed into toddler freedom as they learned to get out of bed whenever they wanted—that, of course, posed new challenges.

When they each started preschool, the first weeks of classroom drop-off were filled with a few tears and leg grabbing; my "babies" didn't want to let go. Of course, elementary school led to a different goodbye at the beginning of the school day. With a wave of the hand, the car door closed, and they walked into school with friends, eager to start the day. Now they are in middle school and we've hit the *"Don't look at me and don't say I love you too loud"* stage, just in case their classmates are in hearing range.

If I'm honest, I admit I miss those younger years. I loved how much I felt needed by my kids, and how I was able to provide for their every need. As mothers before me warned, those years went by in an instant.

One night as I was tucking my kids into bed, my mind wandered to the idea of what the next ten years will bring. Which moments will I find to savor amidst the blurriness of busy-ness?

It was then I created a recipe...a recipe for a nourishing life—the recipe of COMPOST. I quickly realized that answering question of *"What life do I want to create?"* would be hard. How could I unpack a tightly packed schedule? How could I grow our connection to each other in an intentional way?

Gardening together with my family started to give me the answers. Gardening illuminated the ingredients necessary to build a nourishing life. Gardening showed me that *compost* was not only important for my garden, it was important for my life. I started by identifying my purpose and the things that made life meaningful to me.

Mapping all of this out on paper allowed me to visualize and clarify my intentions. I needed more balance so I could savor moments with my family. I was choosing to live on purpose, leaning in to my calling of blending the idea of healthy living with spirituality. I was saying "yes" to the things that mattered most.

I started to develop an attitude of gratitude. While that might sound cliché, it has created a sense of contentment and joy in my days. I started using recipe cards as a format for my journal, because each time I write on them, I am contributing to *my* ultimate recipe. Slowing down and savoring the moments became ingredients in the recipe—a recipe that contributes to a legacy where I will know I have lived a full and nourishing life.

Next, I recognized that I'm a better mom when I take care of my mom-self. I needed some margins or white space in my schedule to nourish myself, moments for me as a mom. It's so easy to fall out of this habit, but when I established this white space for myself, I found I was nourishing my soul and I was better equipped to nourish my family.

To find that space, I needed to prune some things away. I knew I needed to let some things go in order to focus on my intentions. Saying "no" has never been easy for me to do, but I am allowing myself to feel the pain of the prune because I know that pruning will bring new growth.

I am saying "yes" to the things that give life to my intentions. When I analyze a new activity or request based on my time, energy, and talents, I am able to discern if the opportunity will contribute to balance, both at home and in my career. Will this activity allow me to savor moments with my family? Or will I miss something big that I won't be able to see again? Does it fit into my true purpose and intentions? Or would my time be more wisely spent on other activities? Remember, pruning and removing weeds isn't always easy, but it provides space for the more desirable plants to grow.

In developing this recipe to a more nourishing life, I was creating a more purposeful life that was more balanced and not so overwhelmed with what others wanted me to do. I was creating a recipe for a life that matched my values, and it became clear which tasks were the most important for me to spend time on. I started to live on purpose with my values defining everything I was doing.

Surrounding myself with people who help me grow is an essential ingredient to the recipe. The "compost people" we surround ourselves with defines who we will become. Who did I want to be like? I wanted to be kind, humble, considerate, and loving. To reinforce this, I continue to seek out people who want to help others, and not people who just want to help themselves.

Finally, I couldn't just create the recipe without testing out the process. I wanted to experience the ingredients working, making mistakes along the way, and adjusting. I'm still trying to get it just right, but creating a personal recipe of a nourishing life is like gardening. It is a process we learn from over time, and a process that continues while we live and love and laugh along the way. It's a process that won't end until our dying days.

I fell in love with gardening at a very young age and I believe it's led me to where I am today. The Down to Earth, gardening dietitian. I hope that in sharing my journey with you, I have helped you map your own path...for my intention with this book was just one thing...to help *you* create the recipe to a more nourishing life.

Gardening together with my family is one way I've created this recipe because of the many moments it has allowed me to savor with my family and the food it nourishes us with. Gardening together with my family has allowed me to nurture my legacy...a legacy that includes cultivating memories that will build lasting connections. A legacy that includes planting seeds and watching them grow. A legacy that waters and nourishes these seeds so they become strong. A legacy that includes harvesting the fruit of a more nourishing and meaningful life.

Create *your* recipe to a nourishing life:

Take a look at your life in ten years, what do you want it to be like?

What intentions are planted in your heart right now that need to come out and grow?

What ingredients are essential in your recipe to a more nourishing life?

Create that recipe now.

APPENDIX

Values Worksheet

Knowing what matters to you most is a clue to knowing your values. If you have ideas on what those words might be, jot them down here:

Here is a list of common values. Decide what is the most important by circling any of the single words that appeal to you. They are grouped in categories, but feel free to circle just one word out of the category.

- Adventure/Thrill/Risk/Travel
- Balance/Simplicity
- Beauty/Home/Traditions/Nature
- Influence/Encourage/Make a Difference/Be of Service
- Creativity/Freedom
- Discover/Learn/Grow/Sense of Purpose
- Educate/Teach
- Enjoyment/Fun/Pleasure
- Expert/Excellence
- Faith/Spirituality
- Health
- Lead/Inspire/Responsibility
- Relationships/Family/Friends
- Sensitivity/Compassion
- Wealth
- Win/Accomplish/Success

Now, narrow your list to your top five most important values:

Once you know your values, everything becomes clearer. Be intentional with your decisions by measuring your "yes" or "no" against your values. When you focus your time and energy on things that fit within your values, you will feel and be your best!

When I first discovered my top five values, I used a simple tool called the *Values Card Deck*, a product my friend Chere Bork, put together. It's a visual tool that can help you to decide what matters most because you can sort the cards into categories: very important, somewhat important, and not at all important. Using these cards can be fun to do with your husband or even your kids.

You can find the card deck at www.cherebork.com/products.html.

GARDEN TOOLS

There are some basic tools you will need to get started. You can find these tools at any garden nursery, large box store, and even at garage sales:

A garden shovel with a rounded edge. This type of shovel can dig into the ground and break up the soil. It can also scoop soil, compost, or whatever else you need.

A garden hoe. This tool helps you loosen soil and makes weeding a cinch. My kids always want to use this tool for some reason, so you may want to get two! Let the tool work for you—just lift it and let the blade come down into the soil, then simply pull back to loosen the soil.

A garden hand trowel. This is a small hand shovel used for planting and maintaining just about everything in your garden. You can use it to dig holes for plants, loosen soil, and remove weeds.

Hand pruners. Helpful when trying to prune stalks of plants or cut off diseased areas, hand pruners can help you maintain your plants without harming them.

A rake. A rake is helpful when you are working to smooth the soil. After the first garden tilling, there may be trenches or spots where the soil is uneven. A rake can help smooth out the surface to allow for better drainage and therefore, create healthier plants!

A bucket, hose, or watering can. Water is essential to the garden! And watering during the driest days and weeks of the summer, will be important to keep plants healthy.

Plant markers. These can be as basic as painted Popsicle sticks or rocks, or something fancier that you might find in the store. This is an area to get creative with the kids and have them help make something that is weather resistant and safe for the soil.

Gardening gloves. While not necessary, they are nice to have, especially when working to weed out any prickly weeds like thistles.

Digging a Garden Space

Safety first. Call the underground locator company in your community who will survey for pipes or lines that could prohibit having a garden in your space.

Lay it out. Grab a tape measure, four thin stakes or sticks, and a roll of string or twine. Outline the area where you wish to plant your vegetable garden. You may wish to use some white spray paint to outline the shape since you will need to remove the stakes and string for digging.

Dig in. Remove the string and, using a sharp, square-edged shovel, cut along your painted line, going five inches into the soil. Moist ground will be easier to dig, so you may want to dig just after a rain—or water your garden location the night before.

Remove the sod. Next, use the shovel to cut the turf into strips, and then cut the strips into easy-to-handle squares. Force your shovel under each square and lift. You can discard the sod or use it to fill in bare spots on your lawn.

Loosen the soil. With the sod removed, use a shovel to loosen the soil to a depth of 8 to 10 inches. I highly suggest using a tilling machine for this process!

Level the garden. With a rake, level the loose soil, being careful not to pack it down with your feet. Pick out any rocks, roots, and weeds. Create a one foot wide walkway down the center to allow easy access to the garden.

Fertilize the soil. You can now to "top-dress" with three inches of compost or pasteurized manure, then add fish emulsion and liquid kelp.

Plant your garden! Use your garden planner to decide which plants go where. Tall plants and staked plants should be on the north side, so they won't shade shorter plants. Use the spacing guidelines on the tag or seed pack to determine how far apart they should go.

Water in those plants and seeds. Give your new garden a gentle but thorough watering soon after planting, so your young plants won't wilt.

Nutrients for Nourishing Your Garden

Once you have completed a soil test, you may notice lower levels in one of three nutrients—nitrogen, phosphorus, or potassium. Below is a list of organic ingredients to add to your garden. Purchased fertilizers also may also be used, just be sure to note the percentages of N-P-K, or Nitrogen, Phosphorus and Potassium, and use the recommended amounts noted on your soil test. Here is a list of ingredients to add these nutrients back to the soil:

Nitrogen is needed for plant growth, lush leaves and stems, and dark green foliage. You can find nitrogen in the following sources:

- Composted manure
- Worm castings and vermicompost
- Alfalfa meal
- Blood meal (potent)
- Soybean meal
- Green manure—planting a cover crop, like alfalfa, clover, or peas, which infuses the soil with nitrogen, and then tilling these plants into the soil before the planting season begins
- Feathermeal

- Cottonseed meal
- Fish emulsion
- Coffee grounds
- Grass clippings
- Compost

Phosphorus helps plants develop strong roots, flowers, seeds, and fruits. Only supplement your garden if a soil test has indicated levels are low due to potential runoff into ground water. You can find phosphorus in the following sources:

- Bone meal (ground cattle bones)
- Fish bone meal
- Composted fruit

Potassium helps plants resist stress and also helps plants produce fruits and vegetables. You can find potassium from the following sources:

- Wood ash
- Kelp seaweed
- Green sand
- Sulfate of potash

Gardening Books for Kids

Eating the Alphabet by Lois Ehlert

Compost Stew: An A to Z Recipe for the Earth by Mary McKenna Siddals

The Curious Garden by Peter Brown

Growing Vegetable Soup by Lois Ehlert

The Vegetable Alphabet Book by Jerry Pallotta

First Garden: The White House Garden by Robbin Gourley

Garden to Table: A Kids' Guide to Planting, Growing, and Preparing Food by Katherine Hengel

Grow It, Cook It by Jill Bloomfield

From the Garden: A Counting Book About Growing Food by Michael Dahl

Secrets of the Garden: Food Chains and the Food Web in Our Backyard by Kathleen Weidner Zoehfeld

My Garden/Mi Jardin by Rebecca Emberley

The Vegetables We Eat by Gail Gibbons

Conversations to Have in the Garden

1. What do plants need to grow?
2. What do we need to grow?
3. How are plants and our family similar in what we need to grow?
4. What do you think is in the soil that helps the plant grow?
5. Where do we get our nutrients?
6. What happens when we plant a seed in the right soil and give it sun and water?
7. What's your favorite food?
8. Can that food be grown in the garden?
9. What are you looking forward to harvesting?
10. What do you think we can make in the kitchen with that food?

Notes

CHAPTER 1

1. Neumark-Sztainer, D., Berge, J., et al. (n.d.). University of Minnesota Project EAT Study. Retrieved from: http://www.sphresearch.umn.edu/epi/project-eat/

CHAPTER 2

1. Carney, P.A., Harmada, J.L., et al. (2012). Impact of a Community Gardening Project on Vegetable Intake, Food Security, and Family Relationships: A Community-based Participatory Research Study. *J. Community Health. 2012 Aug; 37(4): 874-881.* Retrieved from: http://www.ncbi.nlm.nih.gov/pmc/articles/PMC3661291/

2. Helm, S., Stang, J., Ireland, M. (2009). A Garden Pilot Project Enhances Fruit and Vegetable Consumption among Children. *J Am Diet Assoc. 2009;109:1220-1226.* Retrieved from http://www.andjrnl.org/article/S0002-8223(09)00458-1/pdf

CHAPTER 4

1. Carney, P.A., Hamada, J.L., et. al. (2012). Impact of a Community Gardening Project on Vegetable Intake, Food Security and Family Relationships: A Community-based Participatory Research Study. *J Community Health. 2012 Aug; 37(4): 874–881* Retrieved from http://www.ncbi.nlm.nih.gov/pmc/articles/PMC3661291/

2. Helm, S., Stang, J., Ireland, M. (2009). A Garden Pilot Project Enhances Fruit and Vegetable Consumption among Children. *J Am Diet Assoc. 2009;109:1220-1226.* Retrieved from http://www.andjrnl.org/article/S0002-8223(09)00458-1/pdf

3. American Institute of Cancer Research. (2016). Foods that Fight Cancer. Retrieved from http://www.aicr.org/foods-that-fight-cancer

CHAPTER 5

1. Kalich, K., Bauer, D., and McPartlin, D. (2009). *Early Sprouts.* St. Paul, MN: Red Leaf Press

PHOTO CREDITS
www.123RF.com

Mom and daughter: Cathy Yeulet
Legacy hands: Nagy-Bagoly Ilona
Child holding carrot: maximkabb
Three children with vegetables: Sergiy Bykhunenko
Teens cooking: iodrakon
Herbs in pots: Mornay Van Vuuren
Arugula: Svetlana Kolpakova
Broccoli: fpwing
Beans: Danil Chepko
Cabbage: Denys Prokofyev
Cantaloupe: Svetlana Foote
Carrots: Peter Zijlstra
Cauliflower: lsantilli
Celery: Svetlana Foote
Corn: Maksym Narodenko
Cucumbers: belchonock
Eggplant: Valentyn Volkov
Honeydew: Nat Chantrakool
Kale: Peter Zijlstra
Kohlrabi: Valentyn Volkov
Leek: Peter Zijlstra
Lettuce: Maxfx
Onions: piksel
Parsnips: Konstantin Iliev
Peas: Oleg Dudko
Peppers: Monika Adamczyk
Potatoes: Vaclav Volrab
Pumpkins: Elena Veselova
Radishes: belchonock
Rhubarb: Monika Adamczyk
Rutabaga: Rawan Hussein
Scallions: fotogal
Spinach: Nikola Bilic
Swiss chard: sedneva
Summer squash: belchonock
Winter squash: Elena Schweitzer
Sweet potato: Govindji Patel
Strawberries: Juri Semjonow
Tomatoes: Elena Elisseeva
Turnips: yurakp
Watermelon: serezniy
Girl with garden box: Mykola Velychko

ABOUT THE AUTHOR

An award-winning dietitian, Jen Haugen, RDN, LD is a mom, nutrition communications consultant, writer, speaker, and school nutrition dietitian. Known as the Down To Earth Dietitian on www.jenhaugen.com, Jen specializes in writing and photography with the goal of encouraging moms to create the recipe to a nourishing life through food, family, and faith. Jen also works with clients in nutrition communications creating content, developing recipes, and social media engagement.

Her own gardening seed was planted as a young girl when she spent spring, summer, and fall planting and harvesting fresh produce from her family's farm. She transplanted that knowledge into creating an award-winning garden for kids at Hy-Vee, a nationally recognized supermarket chain in the Midwest, during her six years as a retail dietitian. Jen developed and taught more than 100 gardening and cooking classes for kids, making a significant positive impact on eating habits in families across the community. This program quickly went company-wide due to its success, leading to more than 100 gardens for kids across an eight state area. As creator of the program, Jen authored a complete garden manual for the supermarket dietitian that included lesson plans and recipes. Jen also developed and led training for more than 200 company dietitians.

Jen holds a Bachelor of Science degree in both Dietetics and Food & Nutrition, graduating with high honors, from Minnesota State University at Mankato. She completed her dietetic internship at Mayo Clinic in Rochester, Minnesota, where she later worked as a clinical dietitian for seven years after the internship. In 2012, Jen received the Emerging Dietetic Leader Award from the Minnesota Academy of Nutrition and Dietetics for her work in nutrition promotion through media and gardening programs for kids.

Jen recently delivered a TEDx Talk, "How Moms Can Change the World," featuring ideas for moms to impact the health of their kids through gardening and cooking together.

Jen currently holds the Greater Minnesota Academy of Nutrition and Dietetics Spokesperson position and has extensive media experience including being a weekly columnist for more than five years, contributing and appearing in a weekly cooking segment for more than five years, and writing for national websites and magazines.

Jen is a member of several dietetic practice groups including Nutrition Entrepreneurs (where as newsletter editor, she helped obtain the honored 2015 APEX Award for Outstanding Newsletter), Food and Culinary Professionals, Dietitians in Business and Communications, and School Nutrition Services. Jen is also a member of Common Ground Minnesota, an organization working to start the conversation between the women who grow food and the women who buy it. She resides in Minnesota with her husband and two children.

Social Media Contacts

Pinterest
@jenhaugen99

Twitter
@jenhaugen

Instagram
JenHaugenRD

Facebook Author Page
www.facebook.com/JenHaugenRD/

Facebook Book Page
www.facebook.com/themomsguidetonutritiousgardening

TEDx Talk—How Moms Can Change the World
www.jenhaugen.com/about/tedx-talk-how-moms-can-change-the-world/

You Tube Channel
Jen Haugen, RD, Down to Earth Dietitian
www.youtube.com/user/JenHaugenRD